DO MANAGERS
REALLY KNOW
HOW TO MANAGE?

DO MANAGERS REALLY KNOW HOW TO MANAGE?

How to Lose or Keep a Good Hard Working Employee

Eden Rosen

To order additional copies of this book, contact:
Xlibris Corporation
1-888-7-XLIBRIS
www.Xlibris.com
Orders@Xlibris.com
3144

CONTENTS

ACKNOWLEDGEMENTS

Thanks to all of you who contributed to this book and for your support. As promised your anonymity is being preserved. Thanks again for all your help.

This book is dedicated to all the bosses who do not know how to effectively manage their employees, thereby giving me the reason for writing this book.

This book is also dedicated to all the great bosses who showed me the right way.

PREFACE

Do managers really know how to manage? How does someone become a manager? Why is that person in a position of authority? Does he or she know how to deal with people? These questions and countless others have been asked by employees over and over.

Being a manager or boss requires more than having business sense. Some bosses do not even have that. A manager/employer also needs to know how to effectively deal with many different personalities, a skill many of them unfortunately lack.

Anyone can be an employer. If you decide to open your own business and hire people to work in your establishment, you are an employer and in a position of authority. You may have great business savvy but have you taken any courses in preparation for dealing with difficult employees or people in general? Psychology courses would be an asset or perhaps it just narrows down to treating your subordinates and co-workers with respect and as human beings.

This book is not intended as a license for employees to take advantage of their situations. I wrote it to show owners and managers there are better ways of dealing with employees, as well as the negative effects their behavior can have on the company (profits, morale, etc.).

Although the approach set forth in this book may not work in every situation, remember to treat people the way you would like to be treated.

INTRODUCTION

"Do Managers Really Know How To Manage?"

For those Americans who have been laid off or let go, an employer should make the effort to handle that situation with as much empathy as possible.

In one company, a manager waited until Monday to inform his employees of layoffs. Why? He cared enough about his employees to let them enjoy the weekend. On Monday, the layoffs were discussed and two employees decided to leave voluntarily. In this case, everything proceeded without incident.

In another example, a business owner had to dismiss an employee. He hired her, not realizing she did not have the typing speed necessary for that position. He cried when he let her go a week later and gave her a few extra days severance pay. She had worked for him a little more than a week.

Granted these actual examples may not work in every situation. However, the point is that a manager should have empathy in dealing with such difficult decisions. Remember, it is a very scary situation which could lead to a loss of self-esteem, fear, desperation, etc.

For those Americans who are lucky to still have a job, they spend most of their waking hours working to feed and clothe their families and/or pay bills. Going to work should be as "pleasant" an experience as possible. Unfortunately, most of the time it is not.

Employees have to contend with increased workloads, longer hours, and salary cuts. Sometimes it is a constant struggle to survive. Workers are having problems coping with increases in the volume of work and decreases in salary. To make matters worse, employees may also have to deal with bosses who manage by intimidation or humiliation.

It is not difficult to keep an employee happy and productive, and it can happen without giving away the store. How? Employees should be treated as human beings! Remember, "attitude" starts at the top and "trickles" down. Due to the above belief, I wrote the following article titled, "Ten Sure Ways To Lose (or Keep) A Good Hardworking Employee." It was published in April, 1992 in a local magazine, "Mind's Eye."

The publisher received a lot of phone calls from employees asking for more copies of the publication. Most of them were afraid to let their bosses know how they felt for fear of losing their jobs. By asking for additional copies to be left open on their desks, someone else would become their spokesperson.

This article and a rebuttal letter, refuting a previous commentary, was also sent to the editor of a local paper. Although "Ten Sure Ways" was not included due to space constraints, the letter was published. The writer of the original article called to inform me that my letter had been published. During our conversation, he mentioned he was glad I wrote it and that he even had a bad boss at one time.

"TEN SURE WAYS TO LOSE (OR KEEP) A GOOD HARDWORKING EMPLOYEE"

1. If you want an employee's respect, treat the employee with respect. Don't humiliate or take advantage of your employee. It makes you look small. Respect is earned; it is not a right or a privilege.

2. As an employer, take responsibility for your own actions and errors. Don't blame the employee for something that is not his/her fault. Don't be sarcastic or yell at your employee if he/she does make a mistake. It is not professional. After all, we are all human. If you are an employer, taking pride in your job or company is one thing but don't be obsessed with perfection. It's petty and

shows your insecurities. By the same token, don't tell the employee (even jokingly) you demand perfection. Nobody's perfect, not even you. There are going to be mistakes in a busy office.

3. Don't treat the employee like he/she does not have a brain and then expect the employee to make the right decisions all the time. If you treat the employee like he/she is stupid, you may find the employee acting that way. Perhaps you've heard of the self-fulfilling prophecy. Don't patronize your employee. Never talk down to an employee or insult the employee or his/her intelligence. If you think the employee does not understand something, encourage him/her to ask questions or to come to you for guidance. There is no such thing as a stupid question. If the employee does not feel he/she can talk with you, you will have alienated the employee, defeating your whole purpose for hiring the employee in the first place.

4. A good manager delegates but he/she also knows what and how much to delegate. Don't over delegate responsibility or work. One of the duties of management is the handling of problems employees can't handle by themselves. Don't tell an employee that you believe in team work and lay most of the work and responsibility on the employee's shoulders. If you have to give an employee added responsibility, compensate the employee for it. If you can't do so financially, at least treat the employee with respect and consideration. Employees want and need more than just money.

5. Don't insinuate the employee doesn't do any work or ask the employee what they did all day. Just because the phones aren't ringing off the hook, doesn't mean the employee wasn't busy. You may not be aware of everything an employee does to help make that particular department run smoothly. Good employees always put 100% (if not more) of themselves into their jobs. Genuine appreciation, consideration, and respect by an employer goes along way.

6. Unless an employee is hired as a personal assistant or personal secretary, don't ask an employee to do your personal things. If you

have to ask you employee to do a personal letter or errand, ask him/her to do you a favor and that you appreciate it. Don't pull an employee off work-related items to type personal letters and then ask why the work has not been completed.

7. If there is a problem which can't be resolved, don't dismiss the employee by telling him/her that he/she is wasting your time or to go back to work. At least, if nothing else, validate the employee's feelings of frustration and actively listen to what the employee has to say.

8. Try to be consistent when making decisions. Don't tell the employee one thing one week and then change your mind the next week. Your employee is not a mind reader and should not have to second guess what you want or expect because of your inconsistencies. If you have to change a decision you previously made, at least give the employee a logical reason for doing so. Being inconsistent and illogical is both confusing and frustrating for the employee.

9. If an employee has to stay late or take (no matter what the work is) home after regular business hours, acknowledge the employee's extra effort. In the case of an exempt employee, verbal appreciation, or in the case of a non-exempt employee either time off or overtime pay would be added incentive.

10. A good rule of thumb: before opening mouth, engage brain. Make sure you have all the facts before accusing an employee.

CHAPTER ONE

"RESPECT"

If you want an employee's respect, treat the employee with respect. Don't humiliate or take advantage of your employee. It makes you look small. Respect is earned, it is not a right or privilege.

A boss who manages by intimidation, lies or makes remarks regarding an employee is not professional and does not command respect from the employee.

The following are examples of the non-professional behavior of managers:

An employee told me about an experience she had at one company. Although music was played in most of the offices and outer areas, there was a room where some of the clerical support worked. The music was not piped into their room.

The employee brought her radio into work. The volume was kept at a minimum so it would not disturb others. In fact, everyone traded off listening to their favorite stations. However, every time she went to lunch, the supervisor came into the room and shut it off without ever saying anything.

Finally, after playing this game for a week or two, the supervisor called the employee into her office. Granted the worker should have asked permission, but by now it was too late to do so. During the conversation, the employee explained that certain kinds of music contributed to productivity and since the outer offices had music, the inner offices should also have had it. The supervisor did not want to listen and told her that the radio was disturbing everyone. However, this was not the case. Shortly thereafter, she informed the person who referred her and found another job. The individual, who also recommended her, later apologized.

Was there a better way to handle this situation? Yes! The supervisor should have spoken to the employee in the beginning instead of waiting and playing games. Unfortunately, by the time the supervisor discussed the incident with her subordinate, the worker was experiencing a personal problem and going through a rough time due to a death in the family. She should have validated the employee's feelings by saying, "I know this is a difficult time and I feel uncomfortable bringing this up, but I would appreciate it if you could take your radio home." She could have listened to the employee and then given a rational explanation for the decision, which she did not do. However, it is not a good idea to criticize or play "mind games" with the employee who is in the middle of a personal crisis, for obvious reasons.

If this situation had been handled properly, the problem would have been resolved immediately, and the employee would still have respected the supervisor.

The next example concerns a supervisor who managed by intimidation and was not respected by her employees. Instead, she was feared by almost everyone in her department. She pushed her staff to the limit with disastrous results. She alienated them and turned a very loyal and hard worker into a person who rebelled. The employee, who used to come in early or on time, began to come in late.

How did the supervisor alienate or intimidate her employees? One day, an employee had to order an inspection report for the underwriter. She looked at the guidelines and proceeded to order it. The next day the supervisor approached and asked why she had ordered an inspection report. The employee tried to explain that she had followed the guidelines for the amount of insurance and age of the person. The supervisor did not want to listen, cut her off in mid-sentence, and told her to cancel it, which she did.

A few days later, the supervisor again approached the worker and asked why the inspection report had not been received. The employee reminded her about their conversation. The supervisor became very upset and vehemently denied the fact she told her to cancel it. The employee was also upset and was correct in ordering the report. Although she knew the conversation would get back to the supervisor, she decided to speak to the underwriter about the incident. She obviously could not talk to the supervisor. She wanted the underwriter to know the truth. The supervisor continued to intimidate and discipline her for every little infraction real or imagined.

The employee tried speaking to her supervisor's manager but to no avail. The manager did not care how she managed as long as she got the job done. Unfortunately, in spite of the manager's beliefs, the supervisor was not getting the job done. Employees were becoming physically and emotionally ill due to stress. Shortly thereafter, the employee gave notice. The supervisor asked her how it felt to be pushed into the pool and find she could swim. However, in reality, she had pushed her out the door. The employee filed for unemployment and had to attend a hearing. The company had contested the claim. Although the supervisor denied the incidents, the worker won her case. (This path may not work in every situation and should be taken only as a last resort.)

The employee's previous manager apologized to her for not saying anything beforehand. If the employee knew their "management style" was so dysfunctional and that they bullied the workers, she would not have accepted the position.

Managers need to recognize employees' needs and what motivates them. Not all workers should be, or need to be, pushed. At any rate, they do not need to be intimidated so they act out of fear, not respect. In this case, a better way would have been for the supervisor to discuss the guidelines and the situation with the employee. As soon as she learned she was wrong, she should have apologized. However, by denying she told the employee to cancel the report, the supervisor made the situation worse.

Sometimes a supervisor or co-worker will intimidate an employee because the person feels insecure about his or her position in the department or company.

For example, an employee received two promotions in a short period of time. After the second one, the supervisor's attitude changed. The supervisor found fault with the employee's work, constantly made snide remarks, and made her miserable.

One day, the employee decided to risk her position in the department and end the harassment. Sensing possible feelings of insecurity or jealousy from the supervisor, the worker talked to her while they were alone. She stated that she did not want and was not after her job. After the conversation, the supervisor's attitude changed for the better and there were no further problems.

In this case, the employee took the initiative, a major risk, and resolved the issues. She could not ignore the intimidation and had to change the situation. However, should the supervisor have admitted her feelings and discussed how she felt rather than intimidate the worker? Before you answer the question, consider the fact that not many managers or people in general have the courage to discuss or admit their true feelings. Instead, they act out their hostilities, increasing the staff's level of stress or by making life difficult for their co-workers.

If you cannot discuss your true feelings with the employee, at least try to realize and admit what your feelings are to yourself. It is not easy, but you will be stopping negative/non-productive behavior before he or she asks you to stop.

One employee had a problem regarding her assistant manager. The employee asked a customer if she was being helped. She replied she wasn't. The worker assisted her and carried $200.00 worth of clothing to the cashier who was also the assistant manager. After she had rung up the sale and the customer had left the store, the supervisor told the employee that she had been waiting on that individual, which was not true. The employee explained that she had asked the customer if anyone was waiting on her and that she said no. The assistant manager did not seem upset (at least) outwardly.

In this incident, another customer purchased approximately $400.00 worth of clothing. As in the previous example, the employee also asked this consumer if anyone was assisting her and she said no. The retail associate began helping the individual who decided which outfits to purchase. They brought the items to the cashier who was also the assistant manager. The employee worked very hard on that sale. However, before the total sale had been rung up, the supervisor told the employee that the customer was a friend, she would take over, and told her to help someone else and/or straighten the shelves. When the sale was finally completed, the amount was approximately $400.00. The employee was angry. The sale should have been hers. Although she did not work on commission, a $400.00 sale would have definitely furthered her career. The employee tried to talk to the assistant manager regarding the two sales but it obviously did not do any good.

The employee decided to talk to the store manager with whom she had a good rapport. The manager explained that her subordinate had a difficult life and did not know how to effectively deal with people. She also said that perhaps her assistant also felt insecure due to her upbringing and that she would speak to her. Unfortunately, it made the situation worse. The assistant manager began to intimidate the employee and make snide remarks. The worker could not continue in that situation and when the manager quit for a better job, she also left. She did not want to work for such a nasty individual who bullied her workers.

The assistant manager had first lost the respect of the employee during the initial incident but, more importantly, she was wrong for "taking over" the sales (remember the customers had said nobody was helping them) and for intimidating the employee. The assistant manager should have discussed the situation with the worker rather than bullying her. By browbeating the subordinate and "taking over" her sales, she did not show respect.

Why the store hired the assistant manager in the first place, I will never know. Why hire someone who does not know how to effectively deal with people and place them in a position of authority? To me, that makes no sense at all.

Employers also show disrespect by taking advantage of the staff. Some managers have been known to ask an employee for a phone number from a file which had been on the desk in alphabetical order. Of course, the supervisor needed it immediately. In most cases, the employee had to stop what he or she was doing, walk into the supervisor's office, take the file off of the desk, and hand it to her. What a waste!

Another example of an employer taking advantage of an employee happens when he or she calls a worker at home after work or during the weekend. An employee told me one of her bosses called her on a Saturday evening to ask if she had a fax number of a certain person because the individual to whom she wanted to speak was not at home. It did not matter if it was work related or not, she did not appreciate the call. Aside from that, the manager wanted her to return the call, which, by the way, was fee-based. The employer called back and the employee had someone relay a message. Although she was sorry to have bothered her subordinate, the call should not have been made in the first place. The manager took advantage of her since she never gave permission to be called at home. Managers do not "own" employees.

As an owner, you have the freedom to come and go as you please. However, you are not being fair to your worker if you come in, for example, at 9:30 a.m., tell her what needs to be accomplished before you leave at 9:45 a.m. and that you will be gone for the rest of the day to take care of (personal) business.

Instead, give the employee enough time to complete the work to your satisfaction. This is especially important if a problem arises which commands your attention during those crucial fifteen minutes.

By the same token, if it is busy do not spend a lot of time on the phone making personal calls. You may be the boss but if you come into the office at 11:00 a.m., spend two hours on the phone and plan to leave by 3:00 p.m., your actions do not leave much time for an employee to accomplish everything that has to be done that day.

Your employee, depending on how many hours he/she works, receives an hour for lunch. That doesn't leave much time to complete the tasks at hand. If a problem arises, there will be a delay in processing the rest of the work you wanted completed.

However, even if a problem does not arise, it is not fair to have the employee accomplish everything in an hour because you were on the phone for two hours, wasting time. Perhaps, your employee might not have had to stay late (overtime??) if you were not talking on the phone for any length of time on personal calls. Personal calls should be short and kept at a minimum. If you are the owner of a small company with two phone lines, think about what you are doing. When you spend hours on one line talking about personal matters and your employee is on the other, you may miss important business communications. People hate voicemail. How many times have you criticized your employees or subordinates for doing the same thing?

If you are out of the office on business for the whole day and call the employee with additional information, try to give him or her enough time to complete the tasks without increasing his or her stress by making snide remarks.

One employee told me that the manager called to give her additional information at approximately 4:00 p.m. (her hours were only until 5:00 p.m.). She was waiting for this information so two reports, a letter, and two memos could be mailed the same day. Because she had some questions, the reports had to be reprinted, copied, placed in an envelope and stamped. She knew this task would take longer than an hour and mentioned the work could not be completed by 5:00 p.m. However, the manager assumed that everything was ready, made a snide remark, and told her that the work could be completed before the deadline.

The task was not completed until 5:40 p.m. The employee did not need the additional stress, and the manager should not have assumed anything. (Rule #1-never assume anything!)

In this example, the manager also did not manage time effectively and had crammed too many activities in that day. She did not have to sarcastically ask the worker why the task was not completed. It was not necessary and unprofessional.

These examples show a lack of consideration, taking advantage of your employee and ineffective time management. It is unfortunate that in most companies, employees cannot suggest better and more productive means of running a department or company. A suggestion box and/or including employees in policy meetings, if at all possible, could be beneficial.

Another example of an owner taking advantage is to bring a baby into the office and make staff watch the little one (unless you work for a company that has established a day care center for that purpose). If it is not a necessity for you to bring a baby or very young child into the office, you may want to consider the consequences of your actions before doing so.

First, an office is not child proof, and it is not a safe place for a toddler to play. The child could get hurt. Second, what if the child is accidentally hurt while under the care of your worker? Who is responsible in the event of an accident? Third, it is unfair to lay responsibility of that nature on the employee. Fourth, the individual is being paid to work, not to be a nanny or baby-sitter. If the child makes a mess in the office (papers scattered all over, items pulled off the shelves, etc.) who will clean it? Fifth, bringing a child into the office is not professional and it is distracting and stressful. It is also very difficult for an employee to complete the tasks at hand and keep the child from getting hurt.

Therefore, if the owner asks a subordinate to watch her baby and work at the same time, the employer should not tell the employee that he or she needs to proof better if there is a mistake in a letter. The staff member could have been preventing the child from getting hurt or destroying the office. A simple "I found a mistake" should suffice.

What if the manager is only expecting? If you are pregnant, deciding when to tell your employees is your choice and your business. However, you might want to consider several things before you make your decision. If you are planning to be on maternity leave for any length of time, especially during the busiest time of the season, remember that in your absence your worker will have additional responsibilities and stress. If so, consider hiring someone on a part-time or temporary basis for the time you are gone or give the individual more money for the extra responsibility. Also, if you have decided not to say that you are expecting for whatever reason, you may want to change your mind. It would be much better if your staff heard it from you rather than from someone else. Otherwise, it may show a lack of trust, respect or that you are trying to hide something until, of course, you begin to show your pregnancy.

Humiliating the employee and/or calling him or her names are mistakes managers often make. Doing so also shows a lack of professionalism and respect. Betraying an employee's confidence is only one way. For example, an assistant told her boss that she liked a certain show. Instead of keeping the conversation between them, the manager, who was in her office, humiliated the worker by yelling "and she's got a crush on _____." At the time, the employee was on the phone having a conversation with one of the people involved in the show. She was embarrassed and never said anything concerning the incident. A few months later, the manager again humiliated her during a conversation which took place in front of two strangers. However, this time, she discretely told the manager to stop. These incidents never should have happened in the first place.

Sometimes respecting an employee is as simple as not taking advantage of the individual. What most employers do not realize is that making a worker bring you coffee is exploitive.

However, there are some bosses who do not make their employees do so. The first was a vice-president. When the employee asked him every morning if he wanted coffee, he said that he wanted it only if she was getting a cup for herself. Since he did not expect to be waited on, she brought it to him anyway. He did not take advantage of his workers, he knew how to effectively deal with people, and more importantly, he not only respected his staff, they respected him.

The second boss was a department manager who also poured his own beverage. By doing so, he did not take advantage of his employees.

In retrospect, remember respect is earned and although nobody can take advantage of you unless you let them, it is easier said than done. It is difficult for an employee to speak up in his or her behalf.

Now on to Chapter Two, "Taking Responsibility for Your Own Actions."

CHAPTER TWO

"TAKING RESPONSIBILITY

FOR YOUR OWN ACTIONS"

As an employer, take responsibility for your own actions and errors. Don't blame the employee for something that is not his/her fault. Don't be sarcastic or yell at your employee if he/she does make a mistake. After all, we are all human. If you are an employer, taking pride in your job or company is one thing, but don't be obsessed with perfection. It's petty and shows your insecurities. By the same token, don't tell the employee (even jokingly) you demand perfection. Nobody's perfect, not even you. There are going to be mistakes in a busy office.

Before citing examples, I would like to point out that some managers seem to take credit for the accomplishments of their employees. These individuals think nothing of saying "look what I did" when it was the employee who actually set up the procedure or did all the phone work necessary to resolve the problem. In the former scenario, all the supervisor did was ask a subordinate to set up a certain procedure but took credit for it. In the latter incident, the manager wrote a letter but it was the worker who resolved the problem by constantly calling the company.

An example of a supervisor taking credit for the accomplishment of his/her employee is: In one company, an employee created a pre-screening procedure to eliminate credit applications that had no chance of being approved. The new system would have also improved the company's response time. The supervisor told her the procedure was a good idea but it could not be used.

The employee went on leave for several months. Upon her return, she discovered the company was using it. She spoke to the supervisor who tried to deny it and told her there was no copy available. The employee found her copy and brought it to the supervisor. After discussing it point-by-point, she finally admitted it was the worker's procedure. The employee wanted it to be included in her performance review since it did benefit the company, but the supervisor told her it wasn't necessary. Aside from that, she also discovered that the supervisor took credit for the procedure by telling the department manager it was his idea.

By this time, the employee was very upset and stressed out for several reasons. The first reason was due to the supervisor taking credit for her accomplishment and denying the fact that the procedure had been implemented. The second one was because this individual was doing the work of two people. She was overwhelmed, not because the company was shorthanded, but because one of the other clerks, who could not type, was given special assignments and treatment.

The overloaded employee complained but to no avail. Finally, the department manager insisted that the other clerk do her own typing. However, the supervisor told her to stop typing after the manager left. She also discussed management decisions with this clerk and let her give the orders to the rest of the department which they did not appreciate.

Eventually the entire department complained to the supervisor and threatened to go over his head. Although everyone had to complain, the problem was resolved.

First, one of the worst mistakes managers, employers and/or supervisors can make is to show favoritism. Favoritism doesn't mean complimenting an employee in private for a job well done; it means giving one clerk special treatment over another because you like him or her. Doing so destroys morale, creates stressful situations and eventually causes problems among the staff.

Second, the supervisor should not have taken credit for the employee's accomplishment or vehemently denied the procedure was being used when she wanted it included in the performance review. This is where it should have been without the worker asking for its inclusion. Those actions increased the employee's level of stress and eventually alienated her.

Although the above-mentioned incidents should not have happened, the supervisor could have tried to turn the situation around by owning up to his mistakes and apologizing, not only to the employee and the manager but also to his entire department. Everyone should not have had to complain. Admitting responsibility would have been a major risk, but remember it takes a big person to admit responsibility when wrong. It was inappropriate for the supervisor to show favoritism and take credit for someone else's idea.

These managers took credit for their employees' accomplishments. However, when it came down to taking responsibility for their own actions and errors, some bosses blamed the workers for mistakes that were not their fault. In some cases, the employers did not have to blame anyone. Remember, it is very easy to give away responsibility and very difficult for some individuals to accept it.

Several employees have told me that their bosses blamed them for mistakes they did not make. In one incident, the manager was on the phone speaking with someone she was supposed to have sent information. She never told her assistant to send it. While she was talking, the employee overheard her tell the other individual, "I don't know why she didn't send it out; it was on her desk. I'll ask her about it." Afterwards, she asked the worker whether or not the information had been sent. She had not done so because instructions had not been given. The manager could not say anything more. However, she did not have to blame the worker.

If the boss did not want to admit her own error, she could have covered the mistake by saying "I'm sorry. I don't know why you have not received the information. I will send it today." By handling the error in this respect, the manager is not placing blame.

If she really wants to save face, she could say that the information had been sent and that she is sorry it had not been received. At least she is not blaming the employee in this case, either.

Sometimes, employers will tell the staff in advance they are going to blame them for something that is not their fault. For some unknown reason, they believe this will mitigate the damage. In this case, a boss gave an employee notice that she was going to blame her to save face. Although those in authority may think it will pacify a worker or will help employer/employee relations by telling an individual that he or she will be blamed for something, a better way is to not blame anyone.

In another example, a company could not sway a potential client. The employer told the staff they were not perky enough and thereby lost the account. However, there were other reasons which were a lot more feasible and had nothing to do with the employer or the employees. It was not necessary to blame the workers and it was a wrong decision. It made them feel badly and decreased morale.

In another example, a manager had not taken responsibility for her instructions given to the employee who was entirely blamed in this incident. A particular item was loaned to company A. While company A was using this item, company B wanted to use it and was given permission to do so. The two staff members from the various companies were put in touch with each other to make arrangements.

The employee thought it would be easier without a middleman and updated the manager regarding the status. The manager basically told her everything was fine. On the day the item was to change hands, the employee again updated her boss. She told her no calls had been received regarding the item in question. The manager told her not to worry about it and said that the other individuals were probably busy. She also told her not to call for the status of the item.

However, the employee was worried about it and had a feeling that something was wrong. She called and discovered the item had not changed hands. When she mentioned this, the manager became very upset and eventually screamed at the employee for not following through, giving up control of the situation and waiting until the last minute to inform her of the status.

The worker tried to explain she had updated her and had been following her instructions which were given at the time of the updates, and had followed through. The manager became more defensive, sarcastic, did not want to listen, and blamed her for the entire incident.

Was there a better way to handle this situation? Yes! Perhaps the employee should not have given up control of the situation, however, the manager was informed at every turn. There were no reasons to scream or make snide remarks. The manager didn't take any responsibility, never asked for clarification, and also said she thought the employee was talking about something else.

Instead, this boss should have discussed any concerns with her assistant and she did not do so. She should have listened to the explanation without becoming sarcastic, taken some responsibility for the instructions given, admitted that there was a misunderstanding and that she gave her incorrect information.

The manager should have also apologized and had the sense to thank the worker for calling anyway. Of course in this case, she really believed her assistant was totally responsible for the problem.

However, in researching this book, I spoke to several other supervisors, managers, and business owners regarding this incident. They were of the opinion that the employee was not totally responsible for the problem and stated they would have handled the situation differently.

In another incident, an assistant notified her manager that a large shipment would be arriving on a certain day. It was being turned around and sent to another company immediately.

She told her boss there were going to be extra charges if they brought the packages to the suite. The manager did not want to pay them and had to leave for a few hours during the time the shipment was to have arrived. Prior to leaving, she had given an employee several choices. One option was to have the boxes (several of which were heavy and consisted of different sizes) left near the door, which meant hand carrying all the boxes inside. Her assistant already had a bad back from previously lifting heavy items so she should not have expected her to do so. The other option was to have the driver come back later that afternoon. This was the one the employee decided to use. Unfortunately, the driver never returned and she forgot to get the number of the delivery company. The next day, she was able to obtain the needed information.

The manager became very upset and screamed at her for several days. She even shouted while her assistant was on the phone trying to determine the status of the shipment. The employee was not talking to the right person but she was still yelling.

Nobody I know can think clearly while someone is shrieking at them. The person on the receiving end is only concentrating on the screaming and not on what the person is saying.

Granted the employee should have obtained the number of the delivery company, but it was a mistake and not intentional. A few days later, the manager left on a trip, never mentioning the incident prior to leaving. When she returned, she called the employee into her office three times to discuss the incident.

However, the manager never gave the employee a chance to explain. She told her this is what should have been done, to think things through, that she did not care, and that she had a bad attitude.

Instead of screaming, the manager should have walked away, calmed down and then said she was angry. (By the way, it is okay to say "I'm angry" and then state the reason for your feelings.) As for the manager screaming at the employee while she was on the phone, she probably delayed resolution of the problem. In other words, if the manager had not screamed at her assistant, she might have discovered that she was speaking with the wrong person a lot faster; thereby enabling her to resolve the situation sooner. Shouting at the individual while she was on the phone showed she was unprofessional and had a bad attitude.

Remember, the employee was given the option of having the driver return and that was the one she picked. Her only error was not getting a phone number. It wasn't that she didn't care.

Aside from that, the employee asked the manager if she ever made a mistake. In her reply, she mentioned one example from several years before and how she rectified it. The employee was upset since her boss didn't cite anything more recent and seemed to be obsessed with the error.

The employee shared the story of her boss' more current faux pas. She had called a very high-ranking individual at a company in support of someone who was fired. During the conversation, the manager insinuated she would take a particular action if the person was not reinstated. Afterwards she rhetorically asked, "What have I done?" If she had given thought to the possible consequences of that call, it would not have been made.

The employee wondered (and so do I) how her boss would have wrangled out of that problem if something had gone wrong. The manager had also accused the worker of bad judgment but what about hers?

The worker further stated the manager avoided a confrontation with another person by not returning a phone call for three days because she did not want to be screamed at by this individual. Apparently she did not want to be treated the way she treated her assistant. Ironic, isn't it?

Due to all of these issues, the employee mentioned she almost filed a stress claim but had decided against it.

The previous examples not only show the manager's lack of responsibility for (at least) some of the instructions given, but those, as well as the ones that follow, lead to the next point which is do you yell at your employee or become sarcastic if he or she makes a mistake?

Screaming at someone if he or she does something wrong or becoming defensive when an individual questions a certain decision is unprofessional and it also shows a lack of respect.

I find it ironic that if the manager really thought the employee had such a "bad attitude," would she ask her to return two more times to work for the company on an independent basis? I doubt it.

The independent contractor, who was a former assistant, left when the contract expired because the client gave her more work without extra compensation. This was not in the agreement. Months later, the manager called and asked if she would come back. She said no. This boss told her that one of the employees had made all the changes and things would go back to the way they were if she returned. She politely refused.

Blaming employees, which is what the employer did, for your own shortcomings is never an answer. Doing so only alienates them and decreases morale. This is why the individual didn't want to return.

In one company, the president used to scream at his subordinates for various reasons. Every time employees were summoned to the office, they wondered how he was going to treat them.

Although the staff knew why he screamed, it did not make getting yelled at any easier. One day, one of the employees handed in a departmental financial report, which contained errors. While he may not have screamed at her, he contacted and shouted at one of the managers who then discussed the mistakes with the employee. She corrected the report and brought it to his office where he mentioned the previous blunder again.

Later, this employee had accidentally left a salesman holding on the phone longer than he should have been. He became furious. The worker tried to apologize and validate his feelings, but he did not want to listen and began to scream at her so she hung up on him. He was swearing, and she should not have had to listen to the barrage.

The salesperson called the president who contacted and screamed at the employee and then her supervisor. Eventually things calmed down and the salesperson and president apologized to the worker.

Although the employee made an error in the report and in phone etiquette, nobody had the right to scream at her or the manager. The problems should have been rationally discussed with the worker and her supervisor. Regarding the phone incident, she did not do it on purpose and tried to apologize. Although the salesman was angry, he did not have the right to berate and swear at her. People should learn to control their anger without screaming at each other. Two adults should be able to discuss issues calmly and not wait until hostilities build up for someone to scream.

An example of a supervisor becoming defensive is as follows: A manager, who was leaving town, asked her assistant to videotape programs at home after work. It took five minutes to set up the VCR each time. She had to program the recorder five or six days a week and x number of hours a day for a period of approximately two weeks. This project added twenty-four hours of usage on the VCR. She did not realize how long it would take until she started. By that time, it was too late to ask about overtime or compensation. When the employer returned, the employee asked about overtime, time off or extra money for the usage on the machine. The boss said that because the task only took a few minutes to set up there was no reason to give her anything. The fact that the VCR had been used a total of twenty-four hours in less than two weeks didn't matter.

The manager also became defensive and sarcastically said employees don't have any rights. Although what she said regarding workers' rights is basically true, they do have some, depending on the nature of the problem, according to a representative of a state agency. The employee was so upset that she sent a letter to the CA Department of Industrial Relations. Someone mailed her a form to complete, but she decided not to do so at the time.

The manager should have discussed this situation prior to leaving town. The employee could not ask because she knew her boss would react in a negative manner. However, since they never discussed anything until after the fact, the manager should not have become defensive. She definitely took advantage of her worker and showed unprofessional behavior. She should have also compensated the employee or at least told her that she appreciated the extra effort.

In another example, an assistant was discussing salary, titles, and the job description with her boss. The manager became defensive and sarcastically said that titles do not mean anything. Apparently, however, only her subordinate's was not important. The employer further mentioned that titles should be included when sending a letter to a particular person out of respect for him or her. It was not necessary to become sarcastic or snap at the worker and it showed her unprofessionalism and disrespect for the individual.

In one office, an employee made typing errors. Instead of telling her calmly and rationally (which by the way, was how the situation should have been handled), the manager made snide remarks. The worker mentioned that it is difficult to type a perfect three page letter and then proofread it, when given less than ten minutes. Several days later the employee left on vacation for a week. While she was gone, the manager had to send a few letters. Upon returning, she discovered errors in some of the correspondence. Apparently the manager had not allowed enough time to proof them and had sent the items with mistakes.

If an employee does make a mistake, that does not mean he or she is not trying or doing the best job possible. Unfortunately for some bosses, this is not good enough.

In retrospect, do not take credit for your staff's accomplishments and take responsibility for your own actions and errors. As a manager, recognize the fact that employees are human beings and are not perfect. Therefore, there is no reason to scream at your subordinates or become defensive. As hard as it is for employers to accept, nobody is perfect. Striving for perfection (or as close to it as possible) is one thing, being obsessed is another. If you are, nothing will ever be accomplished and, as I previously mentioned, human beings are not perfect. I am not advocating sloppy habits. All I am saying is that there are going to be mistakes in a busy office.

Now on to Chapter Three, "The Intelligence Factor."

CHAPTER THREE

"THE INTELLIGENCE FACTOR"

Don't treat the employee like he/she does not have a brain and then expect the employee to make the right decisions all the time. If you treat the employee like he/she is stupid, you may find the employee acting that way. Perhaps you've heard of the self-fulfilling prophecy. Don't patronize your employee. Never talk down to an employee or insult the employee or his/her intelligence. If you think the employee does not understand something encourage him/her to ask questions or to come to you for guidance. There is no such thing as a stupid question. If the employee does not feel he/she can talk with you, you will have alienated the employee, defeating your purpose for hiring the employee in the first place.

If you do not let your employee make any or only some decisions, do not be overly critical if he or she makes a wrong one, especially if you have treated him or her like an idiot. Screaming at someone who makes a mistake may make the person lack confidence. In fact, one of the workers (referred to in Chapter Two) told me that it became difficult to make decisions after the manager constantly screamed at her.

By the same token, some bosses do not let staff make decisions and/or they constantly tell them what to say or do in various situations. One worker told me this happened to her. Every time she was on the phone or updating management, the boss would constantly tell her how to handle things. If you always do so, don't be surprised if your employee has problems. At any rate, after treating her assistant as though she lacked intelligence, the manager expected the worker to always make the right decision.

A better way would be to ask the individual what he/she would do in the situation and then discuss the response rationally with him or her. By doing so, you are contributing to the growth of the person.

Aside from managers treating an employee as if he or she was not intelligent, some also are condescending and patronizing. Several examples are as follows: In one incident, a manager had made some changes in a letter, making it difficult to read. She explained them to the employee. After she finished her explanation, she would either say "get it?" or "do you see what I'm saying?" without giving the individual a chance to ask for clarification. The assistant, who was tired of hearing "get it," finally told her, "I'm not stupid. If I don't understand something, I'll ask."

However, in spite of what the worker said, the boss did not get it or see what she was trying to say. The manager continued patronizing this individual. In fact, the employer would often explain something a child could understand and then say "get it?"

If you really think the employee, or anyone for that matter, does not understand something, encourage him or her to come to you for guidance. "Get it?" or "Do you see what I'm saying?" is not how to ask for clarification. There are other ways! One would be to say, "I know I've written all over this letter, feel free to ask questions."

In another example, a manager was handwriting a letter and her penmanship was difficult to understand. She told the employee, "I don't know if you'll be able to read this," and started reading it her.

The manager should have said, "I know this is very jumbled, but take a look at the letter, and I'll go over it with you if you have any questions." Give an employee a chance to see if he or she understands prior to your explanation. After all, you choose your words carefully when corresponding with clients and/or customers, why not employees?

In another company, an employee received a phone call from a customer. Since she couldn't answer all of his questions, she said the manager would call him back. The employee mentioned the conversation to the manager who sarcastically said, "Well, *Name of Employee*, what he was talking about is . . ." She continued to explain what the customer meant in a condescending tone of voice. Luckily, another call came in and the worker was spared any further explanation.

The employee resented not only what the manager said but also the way it was said. The manager should have discussed what the customer meant without being condescending or using sarcasm to make her point.

Another example is: An employee was looking through a report to obtain leads for the department. Later, the manager asked her if there was anything in it. She said, "There was really nothing in the information that could be used." Instead of saying okay, the manager asked, "Are you sure?" Did she think the worker was not being honest? At any rate, since she stated that nothing could be used, there wasn't any reason for the boss to ask for clarification.

From what I understand of the situation, it was not necessary for the employer to ask her subordinate if she was sure. Not only did the manager show disrespect for her worker's judgment, she insulted her intelligence.

The employee was upset since there was no reason for the treatment she received. She always tried to treat the manager as if she had intelligence. She had taken a message for her boss who, after looking at it said, "You have to take better messages. I don't know what you are talking about."

The worker told me what the message was. In researching this book I told several people what it said. They understood.

In this case, a manager gave her assistant a client's address. The employee confirmed the spelling of the street name due to its unfamiliarity. The address also contained the word "Way." The manager also spelled that for her, which was not necessary.

Although she already knew the state, the boss proceeded to tell her that this was in the State of California, and said, "You can put CA." The employee said, "I know." It was not necessary to insult her subordinate's intelligence by saying that CA could be used instead of California.

The employee was upset since this particular manager had previously told her to leave a message on another's answering machine which was not working properly. How ironic!

In one company, an employee was visiting some clients while on vacation. Before she left, the manager instructed her to say nice things about the company. By doing so, she insulted her intelligence. Did the employer really think she was going to say bad things about the company or was she joking? The employee wasn't sure. At any rate, she did not think it was funny, and the manager should have just told her to have a great trip.

In another example, an employee faxed some letters and reports to one of the managers. She told the worker, "I'm sure you'll be confused since we're doing this by telephone." The receptionist told her there was no confusion and that it was difficult handwriting all the changes.

This employer also insulted her intelligence by automatically believing she would be confused. Again, she should not have assumed the employee would become perplexed and given her the chance to ask for clarification, if necessary.

In a similar scenario, a manager was taking work home. The employee gave her a previously used envelope. She told the worker, "I'm glad you used your brain and didn't use a new envelope." The employee felt that this statement was not only uncalled for, it was not complimentary. If the boss really wanted to thank her for picking the right envelope, a simple thank you would have been sufficient and much better. Again, it seems I need to stress that you should carefully choose not only your words but how you also convey them to clients, customers, and employees. If a client or customer made wise or right decision, would you tell them "I'm glad you used your brain?" I think not!

In one company, a boss, who was also a salesperson, felt it was necessary to go over each and every job that came into the shop. Although some of the more complicated ones needed to be reviewed by all parties involved, it was not necessary to discuss those which were simple. Worksheets with information of what was expected could have been completed prior to the beginning of an assigned task.

One employee was upset at her manager's lack of confidence in her ability especially since she had more than ten years experience printing than he had. Her work history was not taken into account, and she felt that her boss treated her as if she lacked intelligence.

The boss should have just brought the job to the employee for review. If the individual had questions, she could have asked for clarification. Instead of discussing it verbally, the employer could have completed a worksheet beforehand which explained what was needed in detail.

Employees' experiences and abilities should be taken into account when giving them work. If you treat any individual like he or she is not intelligent, you may find the person eventually acting that way.

If you have alienated your employee and/or co-worker by insulting his or her intelligence, etc., what good is it? If you continuously do so or do not let him or her make decisions, even the most confident individual may begin to think that he or she is worthless.

In other words, self-esteem will eventually decrease. As one employee said to me, "If I wasn't such a strong person, I'd come home thinking I couldn't do anything right."

Think before you speak; words do sting, especially if your subordinate still cares, is overworked and underpaid.

By the same token, if you don't let your worker make any decisions, if you treat him or her like a child in general or yell at an employee for making a mistake, think of what those actions could do to a person's self-esteem. The individual may find it difficult to make decisions in the future. If he or she is afraid to make decisions because of your words and/or actions, you have defeated your whole purpose for hiring him or her in the first place, which is to provide clerical support and/or assist you in the department and/or company.

Now on to Chapter Four, "Delegating Duties."

CHAPTER FOUR

"DELEGATING DUTIES"

A good manager delegates, but he/she also knows what and how much to delegate. Don't over delegate responsibility or work. One of the duties of management is the handling of problems employees can't handle by themselves. Don't tell an employee that you believe in team work and lay most of the work and responsibility on the employee's shoulders. If you have to give an employee added responsibility, compensate the employee for it. If you can't do so financially, at least treat the employee with respect and consideration. Employees want and need more than money.

If you have not alienated your employee yet, you might do so if you over delegate work and/or responsibility and then refuse to help or drag your feet in solving problem cases. Contrary to what some managers or employers may think, one of the duties of management is handling problems employees can't handle by themselves.

In one company, a manager expected an employee to handle all the routine work and also take care of most of the problems. At one point, she told the worker that they made a good team. However, when she asked for help in resolving problems, the manager made snide remarks or waited a week to resolve the issues. Doing so negated the team effort and increased the individual's level of stress.

If you have to give an employee added responsibility, compensate for it. If you can't do so financially, at least treat him or her with respect and consideration. I covered this issue in greater detail in Chapter One because it is of such high importance and very often forgotten.

The second paragraph shows how an employer treated an employee with respect and consideration and how he handled problems the worker could not handle by herself.

In one company, an employee was working on a few projects. In doing so, she found errors in some of the files and the paperwork quickly became problems to be solved. This took longer than anticipated and she was away from her desk for varying lengths of time. She could not finish her regular work and it began to stack up. She approached both the supervisor and the manager and asked for their help. However, neither one would do anything and basically told her to try and resolve the problems herself. In the meantime, the regular work continued to increase.

One day, while the supervisor and manager were busy, she decided to approach their boss, a vice-president in the company. He sat down with her and together they went through the problem files. He brought those which could not be resolved right away back to his office. Eventually the employee was able to complete everything on her desk. Once her work was current and other concerns arose, she could discuss resolutions with the vice-president, if necessary. In this case, they worked as a team.

The employee never forgot him or how much he had helped, nurtured, and supported her during trying times in the company. This boss not only respected his employees but was also respected by his employees. When he decided to leave the company, she left shortly thereafter.

Remember if you have to give an employee added responsibility, compensate the person for it. If you can't do so financially, at least treat the individual with respect and consideration. I can't stress this enough.

However, in the following example, this was not the case. An employee was given extra responsibility because the boss was going to be out of the office for several weeks. The worker did her best to handle the extra projects. Although the manager acknowledged her efforts eventually, it was the employer's response that was not appreciated. The employee was physically and mentally exhausted and mentioned that to the manager.

Labor Day weekend was nearing which meant an extra day off. Instead of acknowledging the extra effort (more details will be given in Chapter Nine), the manager told her "Well, you have three days to rest." The employee was upset and it was definitely not what she wanted to hear. She was already feeling stressed and that remark did not help matters. In fact, it increased her anxiety. Aside from that, she learned the manager would again be leaving for two more days later that month. She was really furious by that time.

Once the manager returned to work, she should have compensated the employee at the time instead of waiting. If she could not do that, she should have been considerate and respectful. Since the worker told her how exhausting it was to handle the extra responsibility, the manager should have at least acknowledged and/or validated her feelings. (More information on the validation of employees' feelings will be discussed in Chapter Seven.) After all the extra work the assistant accomplished, the manager was not being considerate or respectful when she said, "Well, you have three days to rest."

Some managers don't seem to understand that it takes very little to keep a good hard working employee. They do not realize that doing so can be as simple as compensating him or her fairly and/or treating the individual with respect and consideration.

In this next example, a good employee quit due to a broken promise and lack of compensation, respect and consideration. The individual was a utility clerk. One of the duties was opening the mail, which included applications and checks.

The company lost $10,000 to theft, and the supervisor asked the worker to implement a log-in and security procedure for the checks. She also asked her to postpone her vacation until a new senior clerk could be hired. She further stated this newly created position would eventually be permanent and hers. The employee was excited since it would have meant a substantial promotion.

The employee trained two senior clerks and did the job herself if they were overwhelmed or absent. Six months later, the position was finally created. However, it was given to someone from another department returning from maternity leave. Since company policy required personnel to give the position to the individual who had returned, the employee was not upset until the supervisor told her that she did not get it in a group meeting.

Later, when the employee expressed anger at the way the situation was handled, the supervisor refused to acknowledge their previous discussions. She also constantly asked her to fill in so the other employee could take time off. The worker, who should have had the position, was reprimanded for refusing to take a lateral transfer which would have made things easier for the boss and for complaining about filling in for another employee who quit because of this individual. Apparently, her feelings didn't matter.

The employee no longer felt like doing any favors especially after being told she did not get the position in front of others, the supervisor's denial of the previous discussions, and after working over ten hours of overtime every week. Two months later she eventually resigned, and the company lost a good employee.

The supervisor should have told the employee about the position in private before informing everyone at the group meeting. It must have been very humiliating for the person to find out in this manner. By doing so, the supervisor did not respect her feelings. She should not have denied the previous conversations about the position. Aside from that, she asked the worker to postpone her vacation and gave her extra responsibility which included setting up a new procedure, training two other employees, helping out when necessary and also doing her regular work.

The above-mentioned incidents added to the stress level of the employee who was already overwhelmed because she was working more than fifty hours a week. The individual, who was a team player prior to these and other incidents within the company, began to change and she became someone who was not willing to do any more favors for her boss.

It is unfortunate that managers think that it is okay to overwork employees and as long as they receive a paycheck, it doesn't matter how they are treated. If that is the way you believe and act, don't be surprised if (1) you lose a good hard working employee and (2) you live in a state that compensates for mental stress and a claim is filed against you. I am not advocating either solution. Employees should be able to complain if they are overworked and are upset with the way they are treated. It is up to you to listen and act!

In one company, a manager told an employee to let him know if she had too much work before becoming burned out. It is unfortunate that only some managers feel this way.

However, in most cases, managers overload their employees and tell them to prioritize and not to feel overwhelmed. Aside from that, some bosses continuously ask their staff why certain tasks were not completed. If your employee is doing the work of two or three people and becoming stressed out, it should not matter whether you are a manager or a business owner. You should not feel it is beneath you to make an extra effort to help the individual solve a problem or make one or two phone calls to obtain information. As an employer, if you have time to make personal phone calls or take care of personal things at your desk for hours on end, then you have time to work with your employee as part of a team effort for the betterment of your (or the) company.

In closing, remember that a good manager knows what and how much to delegate and treats an employee with respect and consideration.

Now on to Chapter Five, "What Do Your Employees Do For You?"

CHAPTER FIVE

"WHAT DO YOUR EMPLOYEES

DO FOR YOU?"

Don't insinuate the employee doesn't do any work, or ask the employee what they did all day. Just because the phones aren't ringing off the hook doesn't mean the employee wasn't busy. You may not be aware of everything an employee does to help make that particular department run smoothly. Good employees always put 100 % (if not more) of themselves into their jobs. Genuine appreciation, consideration, and respect by an employer goes a long way.

Do you think your employee doesn't do anything because the phones aren't constantly ringing? Think again because you may not be aware of what your employee does for you. Employees not only answer the phones but depending on their job descriptions, they also photocopy, file, update inventory, and do whatever is necessary to help the particular department run smoothly.

Since good employees always put 100% of themselves into their jobs, it is not necessary to insinuate that they are not working to your satisfaction. Genuine appreciation, consideration, and respect go a long way. In fact, they will want to work harder for bosses who treat them as human beings. Managers who do not treat their employees with genuine respect, consideration and appreciation, may turn a good worker into one who doesn't care. I have seen this happen more often than not, and I will repeat it as many times as necessary.

In one company, a manager asked a new employee to complete a certain task while she was out of the office. The worker was not able to finish the job. The manager asked her if there were any messages. She replied the phones had been quiet. The manager raised her voice and sarcastically asked what she did all day. The employee tried to explain but the boss thought she did not do anything and wouldn't listen. However, this was not the case. The employee had not learned to prioritize the tasks given to her and finished some of the other jobs instead.

The manager should not have insinuated the employee did not do anything without listening to her. The worker was upset because she had at least accomplished some tasks. However, the boss chose to dwell on the project that had not been completed. She eventually turned a good hard working employee into an individual who would rather sit and do nothing whether the work was or was not finished. She did not want to take on any new assignments due to the manager's attitude.

If the employer had appreciated the worker's accomplishments, was not sarcastic, and considered all the facts (see Chapter Ten) before insinuating she did not do anything, the employee would have felt better and there wouldn't have been any problems.

In this case, an employee had a lot of work to accomplish. In fact, the company was just starting its busy season and this particular employee was becoming overloaded. The manager told her on several occasions, "Just wait until you are busy. What are you going to do when it is really busy, or vacation time is over?" The manager was not talking about "vacation" time per se; it was "vacation" time, due to a seasonal slowdown, insinuating that the employee was not busy. However, after mentioning what she was working on at the time of these comments, I could see why she was upset.

The manager did not realize exactly how much the employee did to help the department run smoothly. The employer should never have made the comments and the worker resented them.

In another example, a manager told her assistant, who had just returned from vacation, she could now work hard. Was she joking or insinuating that the employee didn't do anything? The employee wasn't sure but replied she had been working very hard prior to and upon her return from vacation. Joking or otherwise, the statement implied she wasn't doing enough. Comments such as the above are not necessary, not funny and can easily alienate your staff.

In this situation, a manager didn't just insinuate that the employee did not do anything. She actually said so. The worker mentioned something about having more paperwork if a certain deal was arranged. Her boss replied, "Sometimes you don't have anything to do" and sarcastically chuckled about it. The employee was upset since she never took breaks, rarely was sick and worked very hard. Remember, remarks such as these add to the individual's stress level. Don't push anyone so hard that he or she ends up in the hospital or files a stress claim. Since good employees always put 100% of themselves into their job, it is okay if a good worker gets a slight "breather" once in a while (for some people a vacation once a year is not enough). Otherwise, you will have a very stressed out employee. Think about it!

In still another example, an employee told her boss how busy it was while she was out of the office. The manager remarked, "It's always busy when I'm gone." This was not the truth. However, for the most part, it was a very fast-paced environment whether or not the employer was there. Several times, the employee stayed until 6:00 p.m. to finish some of the work. Did the manager think this particular individual didn't do anything when she was in the office? If she thought that, then her thinking needed to be changed since the employee stayed late without overtime pay. There was a constant stream of work and she did not waste time or fool around.

Sometimes, if you don't know how an employee is going to react to a remark you make, the best thing is not to say anything. You could alienate your staff without realizing it.

Genuine appreciation, consideration and respect does not only mean taking your employee out for lunch on Administrative Professionals' Day, giving him or her a birthday party, gift, bonus, or expressing your gratitude once or twice a year. You cannot buy respect (refer to Chapter One) and although the above-mentioned suggestions may help, having genuine appreciation, consideration and respect conveys much more. It also means treating your employee like a human being, not making snide remarks, not humiliating him or her, and being tactful and diplomatic.

If you make snide remarks to your employee, insult his or her intelligence or humiliate him or her, you negate whatever good you are trying to do. Aside from that, your employee will tend to remember the negative rather than the positive aspects of the situation. Do you want to lose or keep your hard working employee? Think about it!

In one example, a manager took an employee to lunch for her birthday. The employer told the worker that she was appreciated, but negated the positive aspects in a matter of a few hours and days.

The manager had found a mistake on a letter and told her she had messed up. Since she had to mention the error, she could have said "I found a mistake" or "I am returning this to you for correction" rather than "You messed up." "I" messages are much better than "You" messages.

Two days later, the manager was explaining something to the employee. The worker told me the instructions were so simple a child could understand what the employer wanted. Yet, she insulted the assistant's intelligence by telling her, "Do you get what I'm saying?" (For other examples, refer to Chapter Three.) There was no reason for the manager to insult the employee's intelligence, and it ruined her day.

If managers constantly insult their staff's intelligence, etc., they will eventually leave, and management will loose good workers. Is it any wonder why employees dislike them or file stress claims?

And now on to Chapter Six, "Personal Errands."

CHAPTER SIX

"PERSONAL ERRANDS"

Unless an employee is hired as a personal assistant or personal secretary, don't ask an employee to do your personal things. If you have to ask your employee to do a personal letter or errand, ask him/her to do you a favor and let him/her know that you appreciate it. Don't pull an employee off work-related items to type personal letters and then ask why the work has not been completed.

In one company, an employer, who wasn't feeling well, asked an employee to pick up his sick child. She did not want the extra responsibility and tried to get out of doing the errand. What would have happened if there was an accident or the child became ill in the car? The owner was very insistent, and the worker eventually picked up the child and brought him home. However the employee was upset and made it quite clear that if anything happened, she would not be responsible. The employee also told him that he would have to pay for cleaning her car if the child became ill while in it.

The only other way the employer could have handled this was to ask a neighbor, a relative, or personal friend to pick up the child. The employee should not have had to run that errand. It did not matter whether or not the individual was paid mileage; what mattered was that she did not want to accept the extra responsibility. Employees should be allowed to say no without retribution by their bosses.

In another company, a manager asked an employee to type a personal letter. She also told her that it needed to be completed immediately and to stop what she was doing. The employee stopped and began complying with the order. However once the letter was finished, the manager asked her why the task she had been working on had not been completed. Since this individual was the one who pulled her off a work-related project to type a personal letter, she should not have asked. The reason should have been obvious. The situation was quickly blown out of proportion and she alienated the employee due to this incident.

The manager should not have asked the employee, in the first place, to type personal letters, or at least, asked her to do it as a favor. She should have told her it was appreciated. Above all, she was wrong by asking the employee why the previous assignment had not been completed.

On the other hand, one employer told me that she rarely asks her employees to handle her personal business. If she has to have her staff do so, she lets them know she appreciates them and does not question why work-related items are not finished. It is unfortunate that more employers do not think in this manner.

Now on to Chapter Seven, "Validation of Feelings."

CHAPTER SEVEN

"VALIDATION OF FEELINGS"

If there is a problem that can't be resolved, don't dismiss the employee by telling him/her that he/she is wasting your time or, to go back to work. At least if nothing else, validate the employee's feelings of frustration and actively listen to what the employee has to say.

Recently I read an excerpt from an article concerning employees' complaints. The writer told the manager that if a worker complained often, he should tell the individual to stop wasting his or her time and to go back to work. I became very upset after reading this advice.

Actually, I was shocked and amazed to learn that managers were being trained to treat their employees in that manner. I wrote to the publisher and editor of the article and sent them a letter and copy of the one I authored. In my correspondence, I mentioned just how important it was to validate a person's feelings in any relationship. They agreed that the validation of feelings was important. How unfortunate that they did not realize that prior to my letter.

If you are a manager or business owner, and you decide to tell your employee to stop bothering you if he or she complains, think again. You will alienate him or her. If nothing else, validate your worker's feelings and actively listen to what he or she has to say. It only takes a few minutes. If you do not have time to immediately discuss the individual's problem, set a time when he or she can talk to you. It is okay to tell him or her, "I understand how you feel" or "I understand your feelings of frustration." It is not a sign of weakness; it is a sign of strength.

Aside from that, you could learn that your employee may not be complaining just for attention or for no reason. More importantly, you will not be alienating your staff.

In one example, an employee had been complaining about several problems which could not be resolved immediately. The first dealt with the quality of the chairs in the department, which were in horrible condition. Management did not try to obtain new ones, and told the employee they were not in the budget. The second one was that the worker had to wait until the new fiscal year, six months from the date of her request. Although the manager did not tell her to stop wasting his time, he said nothing could be done for six months.

In the meantime, she had to suffer. The employee constantly went home with a sore neck, back and legs. The chair was in such horrible condition, that no matter how she sat, it began to cut off her circulation. She complained bitterly. The manager continued to tell her nothing could be done. She became very upset and suffered but not in silence. Finally six months later, all the employees in the department received new chairs.

While the employee appreciated the new one, management should have validated her feelings of frustration and listened. More importantly, it should not have taken six months to find a decent chair. After all, the employee's physical well-being was at risk.

In another health related incident at the same company, management once again refused to take action. In this example, an employee complained about the air conditioning system. The office was freezing in the morning and hot in the afternoon. The employees were constantly becoming sick, and fumes from the duplication equipment and cleaners were filtering through the ventilation system. An employee read articles regarding a phenomenon called the "sick building syndrome" and believed this was the case. The building did not have any windows. The worker complained countless times but management refused to listen. At that time, Cal-OSHA's power was decreased and the agency could not do anything. Shortly thereafter, the employee left the company. She was tired of arguing over such important issues. The company lost a good worker because management would not stand up for its employees.

Approximately one year later, the employee decided to visit the department. She remarked how hot it was in the office. One of the managers told her that the air conditioner had broken down again. This time, however, the repairman had been called. The supervisor told her that the air conditioner filters looked like they had not been cleaned in ten to fifteen years and the moving parts were rusted. How ironic! She just looked at her former boss and said, "I was not complaining for the sake of complaining. I rest my case." The supervisor had proven the point the worker had been trying to convey for six years. Everyone in the building had been breathing all that dirt for years.

Management should have listened to the employee's complaints and validated her feelings of frustration and concern. Instead, they allowed this problem to continue, thereby causing a major health risk, loss of work due to sickness and added to the frustration and stress of all the employees. It is unfortunate that the company had to lose a conscientious worker because management did not care about the health of its employees and did not actively listen to their complaints. What a waste! If only they had listened and made the right decision.

In yet another health related incident, workers were fixing one of the suites in the office building. The chemicals they used filtered through the ventilation system. Several employees from different companies shared their experiences. One employee became dizzy. Others had to turn off their air conditioner due to the strong smell even though it was hot and there were no windows. A third individual, who coughed for approximately five minutes, went home with burning eyes, a headache and became very congested.

The worker complained to two managers. One boss said "I don't know what to tell you" and the other said "Oh, gee." They did not have to deal with the smell and were not in the office for a long period of time.

More importantly, chemicals affect people in different ways. One person may be highly allergic, while another may not have a reaction. Neither manager validated the employee's feelings of frustration and concern. It is difficult to catch your breath when you cough continuously. The smell not only lingered for several days but intensified every day they came to fix the suite.

The managers' responses were not satisfactory. Telling a worker, "I don't know what to tell you" or "Oh, gee" shows a lack of genuine concern for the individual. The ideal solution would have been to send the person home. If that was impossible, a better answer would have been that the managers understood and they were concerned.

In fact, in this same company, an employee received an even worse response in a similar incident. When she complained, the manager sarcastically told her (which did not help the situation) "Well, there's nothing I can do about it." So that makes everything ok? Right? NO! There are solutions. It may not always be ideal, but in all cases, some kind of resolution is better than telling the employee to stop wasting your time or there is nothing you can do about it.

In another company, where chemical smells were more prevalent, the employees were subjected to very strong odors. They tried to close the doors leading to the department where the smells originated, but management quickly rejected that idea and told them the doors had to be kept open. The managers did not validate their feelings. Instead of sending the employees home or outside while management tried to eliminate the smell, they made the staff continue working. Employees were going home with headaches, sore throats, burning eyes and congestion. Management angered and alienated their workers.

If my employees had health concerns over reactions to chemical smells, I would make phone calls to the building manager or company executive to try to resolve the problem. If I could not do so, I would find another solution. Employees should not have to go home stressed out and physically ill. If you do not validate their feelings, you are compounding the problem. Aside from that, even if it costs you a few extra dollars in rent or to fix your company's ventilation system, you will be saving money in the long run. Remember, there are airborne viruses and if workers become ill, it could cost the company much more than a few hundred dollars. Again, if nothing else, at least try to resolve the problem and validate the employees' feelings. It will help!

If the above-mentioned issues were not enough, you can also add to the employees' stress levels by being inconsistent or by not making a decision which could impact them.

Now on to Chapter Eight, "Management Decisions and Inconsistencies."

CHAPTER EIGHT

"DECISIONS AND INCONSISTENCIES"

Try to be consistent when making decisions. Don't tell the employee one thing one week and then change your mind the next week. Your employee is not a mind reader and should not have to second guess what you want or expect because of your inconsistencies. If you have to change a decision you previously made, at least give the employee a logical reason for doing so. Being inconsistent and illogical is both confusing and frustrating for the employee.

If you have to change your mind or a decision you previously made, give your employees a logical reason and don't make unnecessary remarks. Otherwise, it will be confusing and frustrating for the workers and increase their stress levels.

In this example, an employee's family member had to have an operation. The worker mentioned it to the manager who told her that it was okay if she did not come into the office. The day of the surgery, the employee called to make sure everything was fine. The employer told her she could come in late. Remember, however, the boss previously stated she did not need to come into work. The assistant told her that she did not know what time she would be in but would do so to complete some of the work rather than taking it home. She arrived later that afternoon and called the manager who said, "I didn't think you'd be in" and thanked her.

The manager, who was organizing a family member's birthday party, could not cover the office. Two days later, the employee's loved-one had a second surgery and she had to leave early. The manager told her somehow they would work through it. Although the worker needed the money, it was unfortunate that she could not have more time off. She was exhausted from going to work and running to the hospital during the week.

The manager, who added to the employee's level of stress by being inconsistent, should have allowed her to make the decision regarding work. After all, she was experiencing a very stressful situation. Although she appreciated the time off, more hours away from the office would have even been better.

Several months later, the boss allowed this employee, who rarely took time off from work and never took breaks, to leave early for a family member's first doctor's appointment since surgery and her own visit to the physician the next day. The manager wasn't going to be in the office and wanted the phones covered. She changed her mind several times. The employer finally told the worker it was okay to keep the appointments but to return as soon as possible. She said someone had to watch the phones.

At this time, the employee did not have a problem. However, she became upset after the manager's previous remarks. In this incident, the employee left to take the family member to his appointment since he could not drive. The phones were not covered, per the employee's conversation with the manager. When she returned to the office, she called the manager who remarked that it was the busiest time of the year and that the phones should be covered. The employee did not say anything.

The next day, the employee had a doctor's appointment. When she returned to the department, there were two messages on the answering machine. She called the manager and informed her of the phone calls. The employer remarked, "See how important it is to have the phones covered." The employee replied, "Well, one of the calls came in during the regular lunch hour, and I wouldn't have been here anyway." This time, she refused to bear the brunt of the manager's remarks. Needless to say, the employee was frustrated, stressed, and angry.

First, it was the sole decision of the manager who changed her mind several times and decided not to cover the phones. It was not the employee's fault they were not covered. In fact, the employee said she asked her boss if she should try and find someone.

Second, although it was the busiest time of the year and it was important to have the phones covered, the manager's remarks were unnecessary. Aside from that, the irony of the situation was that the boss was going on vacation the following week, leaving the employee with extra responsibility.

The manager was wrong in making those remarks to the employee. Doing so increased her level of stress which was already high due to anticipated extra responsibility.

The manager should have just said, "I have decided not to cover the phones. I would appreciate it if you could please return to the office as soon as possible."

In another example, an employee was supposed to send out a report to a client once a month. One day, the manager told her to wait until she received new information. She complied, and did not send anything for several months. Later, when the employee asked whether or not she should mail it, the manager inquired why the report wasn't sent. The worker reminded her. The manager told her it should have been sent and to begin doing so again. Aside from that, the manager made it sound like it was the employee's fault. Several months later, she ran an updated copy of the report and asked the manager if it should be mailed. Again, she advised the worker to hold off and then later told her to finally send it.

The manager was not only inconsistent but also tried to blame the employee for not sending the report. Perhaps, she forgot that she told her to wait. In fact, most problems occur because the person can't remember what was said five minutes before or several months later. Memos only work if a) the manager or employer is willing to implement that procedure and b) they do not become defensive when their inconsistencies are pointed out to them.

In another company, a manager and an employee were working together on a project. Although the manager was out of the office, they kept in touch. The worker put the needed information in the computer and faxed it to her.

The assistant did not have a lot of time to work on all facets of the project but finished as much as she possibly could. She offered to fax the additional information to the manager who said it wasn't necessary. Therefore, the employee had to read some information from the appendices several times before she understood.

Aside from that, the manager told the employee it was okay if the draft was not finished before lunch. Then she stated she wanted the project out that day. Also, when the manager returned to the office, she sarcastically kept asking, "Well, didn't you read this? Didn't you do that?"

The employee had rushed to complete the drafts and tried to do the best job possible under the circumstances. Besides, the manager turned down a review of the appendices before returning to the office. If those extra pages had been sent, it would have saved everyone a lot of grief. The employee, however, faxed one extra page to the manager which could have helped but doubts it was ever used. Furthermore, there was one specific point that had to be changed, and the manager explained the reasons to the employee. However, when that same item came up again, the employee mentioned it to the manager, who sarcastically replied, "That doesn't matter." Ironically, it mattered a few hours before. Every time the employee made a suggestion, the manager became sarcastic.

The employee left spaces in the draft to fill in additional information that was unavailable at the time. The manager told her there were mistakes in the correspondence. The worker replied that the blanks and spaces, etc. were there for a reason, and she proceeded to explain. She also knew that mistakes didn't matter, since the employer would change the wording several times. When the employee told me what transpired, she further mentioned that when the manager returned to the department, she told her to finish the project as soon as possible. The boss was in a hurry and needed to leave again for personal errands.

As I previously mentioned, if the manager allowed the employee to fax the additional information to her, the project could have been completed earlier.

The manager should not have made sarcastic remarks because it increased the employee's level of stress. The worker not only had to deal with finishing the project but also her boss' sarcasm and inconsistencies. Needless to say, the employee was very stressed due to the entire situation and it did not have to happen.

In another department, an employee wrote drafts for the manager's perusal. Upon review, she said the letters were fine and the worker printed them for signature. When the boss read them again, she told the individual to make various changes. The worker wondered why the boss changed her mind since 30 minutes prior to this, everything was fine.

Several days later, the employer had someone else write other letters which she approved. These were printed for signature. The manager had her change and reprint two of the items. The employee told me the changes weren't due to typing errors.

If you change your mind or decision, please give your employee a logical reason. Doing so really does help. Some managers are obsessed with perfection and have crossed the line between flexibility and inconsistency. If you constantly berate your employee and are also inconsistent, you will either eventually lose the individual's respect or he or she might quit. Stress claims may also be filed against companies if allowed in the state in which they are doing business.

In still another example, an employee told a manager that the fax machine was broken. She told the worker not to do anything. However, several days later, the boss told her, "The fax machine isn't working. You better call and see about getting it fixed." The employee wanted to do that several days before but was not allowed to call for service. In the meantime, nobody could send out anything. The manager, who was the only one who could authorize the expenditure, should have listened to the employee and had it fixed when it was first mentioned. Once permission was given, the employee could research the problem and get it solved with minimum effort and she did so. The telephone line was bad. The manager could have simply told her, please call for service or research the issue and report back to me, etc.

Although this may not be a blatant example of inconsistency, the manager should have listened to the employee instead of telling her not to do anything. It increased the worker's level of stress and wasted valuable days.

In an example, which will be discussed in Chapter Eleven, I mentioned managers who made sarcastic remarks to employees about having the labels and stamps placed perfectly on the envelope. However one of the bosses also told a worker, who made a mistake while addressing holiday envelopes, to "white out" the faux pas. The employee was upset and told her it was tacky.

The employer wanted to save the envelope by using "white out" but constantly criticized the individual for not putting the stamps on straight. Doing so showed the manager was illogical and inconsistent. Aside from that, when the employee was almost finished, there seemed to be more time to put the stamps on "perfectly." This manager told her, "That's the way to do it."

The boss should not have been so obsessed with perfection on one hand and not on the other. If you are, this alone is an example of being inconsistent and is quite frustrating for the staff.

In fact, I have seen mail with stamps upside down and crookedly placed postage via a meter, etc. I am not advocating sloppy work habits; I am saying those things can and will happen in a busy office and/or mailroom. Don't drive your employee to distraction by your inconsistencies or obsession with perfection. There have been articles written on the consequences of being obsessed.

In one company, a manager wanted the employee to take the initiative in solving problems or dealing with changes, etc. However when the worker tried, the manager said that she would handle any changes in status, etc. At one point, the boss told her, "Think

DO MANAGERS REALLY KNOW HOW TO MANAGE?

of how I would handle the situation and then call and ask me." Of course in an emergency, an employee is not going to have time to wait for an answer. If you do not manage by example or have the attitude "don't do as I do, do as I say" and are inconsistent in other ways, your staff may not be able to think how you would handle a certain situation. In the very least, it would make it more difficult for anyone to second guess you. Again flexibility is one thing; inconsistency is another.

In one company, an employee was supposed to invoice another organization for a certain item. She told the manager that she had not sent a bill yet. A simple reply, "send an invoice," should have been the response. Instead the boss replied, "He hasn't been invoiced yet? Everyone needs to be invoiced, as we found out. Send him an invoice today." The worker went to lunch. Upon returning, the manager told her, "I feel funny invoicing them until they receive the item." Although she gave a logical reason for reversing the previous decision, her remarks were not necessary. In fact, sometimes the simplest answers are the best. In this case, as I previously mentioned, a simple "please send an invoice" would have been sufficient. Then the manager could have changed her mind without trying to make this the employee's problem.

In yet another example, a manager inadvertently forgot to sign an employee's check, dated it a few days later and then left for the day. Although she told the worker a few years prior to this incident, that if the 15th fell on a Sunday, staff would be paid on a Monday and if the date fell on a Saturday, payday would be Friday. Of course, it had never been implemented. However, when the employee went to get the check, it was not signed and it was dated three days later. She was very upset because she was counting on it to pay bills.

She called the boss at home and left a message. The manager returned the call, told her that the oversight was not intentional and wondered why she was so upset. The employer also mentioned that previous conversation from a few years ago. The employee replied, "Sure I remember the conversation, but the procedure was never implemented." The manager signed the check and changed the date the next day. A few days later, after putting the assistant through all that extra stress, the boss told her, "If you ever need an advance let me know."

Although not signing the check was accidental, the manager should have understood its importance and reasons for the worker's emotions. The assistant was upset not only due to the lack of the authorized signature on the check but also because of the manager's inconsistency. The employee was being paid on the 15th and 30th and/or 31st of the month then she was told payday would be other dates (depending how payday fell). The manager never implemented the changes, and then without any warning, she dated this particular check three days after the date the employee had expected. Any wonder why she was upset?

Ironically, six months after this incident, this manager told the employee about a similar situation. The only difference was that the first one was not intentional (or at least the lack of the authorized signature was an accident). After hearing the story and the manager's remarks, the worker replied, "It's unfortunate that some employers do that to their employees."

Taking this point one step further, it may be legal (check with an attorney or the labor commission) for a company to hold employees' checks over a weekend or holiday (if payday falls on Thursday/Thanksgiving, for example) but it certainly is not fair. Again, keeping a good employee may be as simple as being consistent and paying him or her on time. Isn't it worth the few extra dollars to you to keep your worker happy? Some individuals live paycheck to paycheck and holding their check for three or four days may create undue hardships and more stress for them.

Think about it! You may want to change your company policy for good reason. Being inconsistent doesn't only mean changing your mind or your decisions. If you treat your employee like gold one day, yet make snide remarks, yell at the individual for making a mistake or insult someone's intelligence the next, you are inconsistent.

It is very frustrating for the employee because the individual won't know if he or she will be praised for a job well done or blamed for something that is not his or her fault.

Aside from that, you are also increasing the employee's stress level. It should not matter whether you are an employer/manager or employee. What matters is what's fair. Bosses can treat a worker well one minute and snap the next, and it's considered a mood swing.

However, if an employee makes a snide remark or snaps at the manager, the individual is considered to have an attitude problem or told to leave his or her problems at the door. This is unfair. Employees can also have mood swings. They get stressed and have bad days as do managers. Why? Because they are human beings. As one employee said to me, "I don't know if I'm going to be praised or put down for every little thing."

There is no reason for such mood swings and/or inconsistencies. You can change if you set your mind to it. You don't want to drive your staff to distraction by changing your mind every two minutes and/or by praising your people one minute and making snide remarks the next. A good hard working employee is a company's best asset and one worth keeping!

Now on to Chapter Nine, "Acknowledging An Employee's Extra Effort."

CHAPTER NINE

"ACKNOWLEDGING

AN EMPLOYEE'S EXTRA EFFORT"

If an employee has to stay late or take work home after regular business hours (no matter what the work is), acknowledge the employee's extra effort. In the case of an exempt employee verbal appreciation, or in the case of the non-exempt employee, either time off or overtime pay would be added incentive.

Does your employee make an extra effort to complete the tasks? If he or she has to stay late, take work home after regular business hours or pick up items on his or her own time, how do you show your appreciation?

Telling your worker how much he or she is appreciated is only the beginning. Don't wait until Administrative Professionals' Day, his or her birthday or when he or she resigns. You should also give compliments when your employee does a great job or goes out of the way to accomplish a task.

Above all, treat your staff with respect and consideration. Also, be sincere when you acknowledge the individual's effort or compliment him or her. If you aren't, you will lose the person's respect and loyalty.

If you finally acknowledge the employee's efforts when he or she resigns, it is too late to say how you feel or convince the individual to stay. If you wanted him or her to do so, you should have thought about acknowledging the employee's efforts or letting the worker know he or she is appreciated prior to resigning.

Do you pay overtime or give your employee time off? Be sure to check the labor laws in your state if you decide to let your worker trade time off or if you refuse to pay overtime. Think about how he or she would feel if you do not acknowledge the employee's efforts and/or do not pay overtime. Several employees told me they had to leave their positions because they felt unappreciated, taken advantage of, or their efforts were not acknowledged.

In one company, there had to be a major exodus before the owner realized he did not appreciate his employees and pushed them too hard. By that time, it was too late. He lost many good employees. If only the owner had appreciated his staff while they were still employed. In another example, an employee had to quit before the manager let her know that she was appreciated.

In a different organization, an employee went to a store on a Sunday to pick up some items for a major project the department was going to be working on the next day. On Monday, she told the manager about the Sunday trip to the store. The boss said, "That's great you did that." Although she probably meant well, there should have been more to the compliment. After all, the employee spent over an hour of personal time at the store on her day off, without being paid overtime. If my subordinate put in extra hours, I would have said thank you for doing that. I really appreciate the extra effort you have put into completing the project and/or paid overtime or compensated the individual in some way. If you were the worker making that trip, I am sure you would want more than a slight acknowledgement of your extra effort.

In one company, most of the employees were given extra work. Management also expected them to come into the office Saturdays or stay late to complete the additional tasks at hand. Since most of the workers were exempt from overtime pay, they should have received verbal appreciation for their extra efforts. The bosses could have said, "We really appreciate all the extra time you have put in" or "Thanks for coming in on Saturdays to finish the additional projects." The employees should have also been treated accordingly, at least emotionally, if not financially.

In the above-mentioned example, however, the employees did not receive any verbal appreciation nor were their exta efforts appreciated. Instead, they received nasty memos from their supervisor and, in spite of the extra work and additional hours, they were expected to be perfect and not make any mistakes. Due to the additional hours, the increased workloads, the lack of fairness within the company (some individuals were given less work), and management by intimidation by the supervisor, several of the workers were forced to quit and no new people were hired to take their place. Several employees filed stress claims. What a shame and a waste of money, time, and effort. No wonder morale was low.

First, I do not agree with management by intimidation. The nasty memos were not necessary, especially when these employees were making the effort to complete the additional work to the best of their abilities.

Second, where was the supervisor's boss? Did the manager approve of the individual's management technique or was the employer so disconnected from what was happening? The organization believed in solving problems through a team effort but even so, managers must make every effort to become more aware.

Third, if the company has financial problems and cannot afford to pay the staff more money, then by all means, managers should treat the employees honestly, fairly and with respect and consideration. In fact, this is how employers should treat their workers whether or not the company is having financial problems. If there are changes pending within the company, management should be honest. It's amazing that bosses expect loyalty and respect from their employees, but will not respect or be honest in return. Employees do not like being deceived or forced to quit due to the "management style" of their supervisors, especially in this economy.

Fourth, increased workloads and the lack of fairness within the company added to the employees' levels of stress. Nasty memos, intimidation, and the pressure to be perfect while meeting unreasonable quotas also increased everyone's anxiety. The greater the pressure placed on workers to not make mistakes, the more they made them, especially if they were tired. Eventually, this led to employee burnout and more stress claims being filed.

Remember that the treatment of an employee, such as acknowledging the person's extra effort, treating the individual with respect and consideration, writing nasty memos and lack of respect can influence morale, thereby having a positive or negative effect on the company's bottom line.

Sometimes bosses have a difficult time expressing compliments. If it is hard to say thank you, show appreciation, or compliment an individual on a job well done, you should try and change your way of thinking. Tell your worker how you feel or give a compliment. However, if you criticize your staff for every little thing and/or are sarcastic when you call attention to errors, the individual will remember the negativism and the sarcasm rather than the positive acknowledgments.

Although this chapter does not contain a lot of examples, it is important to acknowledge your employees' efforts and compliment people on their efforts. Otherwise, if your worker quits for whatever the reason (interpersonal relations, stress, etc.) it will cost your company more in the long run. Training is very expensive, and turnover is very costly. You may want to consider that before you ignore an employee's extra effort or are sarcastic. An employer's market should not make a difference in how staff is treated. Employees should be treated as human beings and, who knows, you may be surprised at the results.

If you believe you haven't lost someone's respect by now, you may not realize that you already have. Think before you speak and be aware that your words and/or actions can alienate an employee, especially if you jump to conclusions or blame him or her before having all the facts.

Now on to Chapter Ten, "The Facts, Please."

CHAPTER TEN

"THE FACTS, PLEASE"

A good rule of thumb: before opening mouth, engage brain. Make sure you have all the facts before accusing an employee.

Employers sometimes have been known to accuse their employees of wrong-doing without having all the facts.

In one company, an employee had to replace a cash register tape. She had removed the used one without any problems. However, when she tried to replace the tape, it would not go in correctly. She could not find a manager and asked another clerk for help. The other worker told her that he knew what he was doing. The next day, an on-call manager found the employee and angrily told her that all the sales had to be rung over because the tape had been put in wrong. He did not have all the facts and did not ask the employee for her side of the story. He assumed she had replaced the tape incorrectly and told her if she needed help, she should have asked. The cashier angrily told him she had asked for help and one of the other clerks had replaced the tape. All the manager could say at that time was, "Oh!"

Was there a better way to have handled this situation? Yes. First, the clerk who had replaced the tape should have been truthful if he did not know how to do so. Although he had worked at the store longer than the individual who asked for his help, it would have been okay for him to say, "I don't know how to replace the tape," if that indeed was the case. Second, the manager should not have assumed facts not yet evident. He should have learned all the facts prior to accusing the employee of wrong-doing.

In another example, a manager called a number which was temporarily being used for something else. While she was on the phone, she never asked the individual to whom she was speaking if the person she needed could be reached there. The manager automatically assumed number was incorrect. She accused the employee of writing it down wrong even though the worker said someone had given it to her that way. The boss tried calling again and discovered it was correct.

The manager should not have assumed the number was wrong or jumped to conclusions before she re-dialed. However, since she accused the employee of making a mistake, the owner should have apologized. Remember, it takes a big person to say I'm sorry, I was wrong or I jumped to conclusions.

In yet another example, an employee had some personal mail sent to her workplace. Granted she should have had the letter sent to her house; however, she did not know the sender well enough to give out the home address. The worker told him how to address the envelope. Unfortunately, he did not follow her instructions, and the item was sent to another department. Although the employee's name was on it, someone else opened and read it. The person who did so was not upset that the worker had received personal mail; he was upset at the contents. He assumed the employee was involved in a conflict of interest situation and spoke to her manager. It was not until she gave her side of the story, did they realize nothing was happening.

However, the worker was quite upset for several reasons. First, that letter should not have been opened by anyone else. Second, several high ranking officials in the company were involved in things, many would consider a conflict of interest. Third, she apologized but nobody else did for opening her mail.

Other examples of employers jumping to conclusions are: In one company, an employee was faxing some information to her boss who was at home. The manager had been receiving blank pages. She called the office and told her assistant that the pages must have been fed in wrong or backwards. The employee stated she had sent the pages face down, which was correct. The manager then replied, "Oh maybe, I put the paper in wrong." The manager did put the paper in wrong. The employer should have apologized for jumping to the conclusion that the employee made the mistake. Better yet, the boss should not have blamed the worker and checked her own fax machine before calling the office.

In another company, an employee received an incomplete insurance document. She told the manager that data was missing. Instead of thinking the people who had sent the paperwork had omitted it, the manager asked the assistant if she remembered to ask for that information.

The employee told me there is a standard letter that is mailed when necessary. She had to stop and look for a copy so she could prove that the information was not omitted.

If the manager did not want to take the employee's word that the sender made a mistake, she should have just asked her to pull the copy she sent. The boss did not need to ask if she forgot to include the information in the letter.

Still other examples of employers jumping to conclusions are: In one department, a manager told an employee to mail a payment on a certain day. She complied. There was a problem with the check. Instead of believing the worker mailed the payment on the specified date or asking her to confirm the mail date, she assumed the assistant had mailed it early. In fact, she said, "You must have mailed it early." The employee told her when she sent it.

The manager, who did not have all the facts, should not have assumed the worker mailed the payment early because there had been a problem with the check. Remember rule #1: never assume anything.

In another company, one of the phones in a certain department rang while the employee was on another line. The manager who was returning from the bathroom walked over to the employee and said, "Don't let the phone ring so long." She told the manager, "The phone only rang three times. Three times is not bad." Without having any facts, the manager jumped to conclusions.

Hypothetically speaking, what if your employee was the only person in the department that day and happened to be in the store room where there was no phone? Would you rather have your employee trip or get hurt rushing to answer the phone rather than let it ring one extra time? Sometimes it is impossible to answer the phone on the first few rings.

In another example, an employee in company A told her manager she received a phone call from a worker from a different company (company B) who seemed upset. This individual (company B) was returning a call which had previously been made to her boss regarding some information. Company A's assistant told her employer about it. Immediately the manager asked her somewhat sarcastically, "What did you say to her?" She replied, "What you told me to say," and further explained what she said. The manager did not think that the reason Company B's employee might have been upset was because she had spoken to her boss. Instead, she jumped to conclusions and blamed her own assistant.

The manager from company A should not have accused her employee of making a faux pas by implying that she had said something wrong. A simple (without the sarcasm) "Tell me what happened" should have sufficed.

Two other examples of a manager jumping to conclusions without having all the facts, thereby blaming an employee for something that was not her fault are listed below.

In the first example, an employee (A) was training a new employee (B). Worker A told B to let her know if she was giving her too much information. B never said anything to A or the manager. A few days later, B went to lunch and did not come back. Phone calls to B were not returned.

The manager asked employee A, "Did you overwhelm her?" A replied, "I told her to say something if I was giving her too much information. She never said anything." Ironically, the day A told B to let her know if she was giving her too much information, the manager was standing nearby.

In the second example, a folder of completed job applications was misplaced. The employee had previously filed the documents in the appropriate drawer. However, someone had taken them out and, without thinking, placed the items in another one. The manager blamed the employee, became sarcastic, told her she had given her the file, and asked her where she had put the folder. However, after several minutes, the manager found it in another drawer on the other side of the desk. The worker told me she would not have had a reason to place the file elsewhere. She told the manager, "I did not put the file in there." The employer sarcastically told her that it did not matter since the file had been found.

The employee was upset. There was no reason for the attitude, and it did matter since she was blamed for the file's disappearance, even though she was not responsible. The manager should not have used sarcasm or accused her in the first place, but since she did, she should have, at least, apologized. It was not her assistant's fault. The manager's response should have been, "I can't find the job application file. I would be grateful if you could help me find it." By blaming the worker and using sarcasm, she closed lines of communication and alienated her.

Accusing employees of wrong-doing before having all the facts increases stress levels as well as decreases morale and productivity.

In Chapter Eleven, I cite more examples of stressful situations and pose the question, "Will Some Managers Ever Learn?"

CHAPTER ELEVEN

"MORE STRESSFUL SITUATIONS

WILL SOME MANAGERS EVER LEARN?"

This chapter cites various experiences, problems and/or examples which could be placed in several categories, are not covered in any of the other chapters, or to drive home a point.

Sometimes employers create stressful situations due to a lack of common sense. In one example, an employer told a client in front of the employee and a co-worker, "I'm training _____. How did she do?"

I think the employer should have privately asked the client how the employee did and then discussed the situation with the worker if there was a need.

In another situation, an employer wanted an independent contractor to do something that was not in the agreement. The contractor said, "I'm sorry, that's not in the contract." The employer said, "I don't care. We all help each other." The manager could have asked her to do it as a favor because everyone was so behind in their workload. The individual only came in for a few hours each day.

I thought a contract was a legal agreement. Helping employees was never part of the arrangement. In fact, there was nothing dealing with that situation at all. Asking the person to do something that was not in the contract could have been construed as a breach of the agreement.

The irony of the situation was that one day the employer was speaking to a client who asked her to do something for free. She hung up the phone and said, "I'm not working for free." Yet, this boss expected the contractor to do things that were not in the contract. How ironic.

One day, the independent contractor came to the office. The door was locked and there was no note. However, she was able to find someone with a key. She mentioned the incident the next day. An employee told her, "We didn't know what time you were coming." The contractor was expected to be a team player but nobody left a note or invited her to meet them at the birthday lunch they were having for one of the employees.

In a span of one to two years or less, this company lost five or more employees. If employers treat staff poorly, they wind up with unhappy, frustrated individuals who quit, become uncaring workers, or worse.

In one company, in the midwest, clerical employees were going home in tears almost everyday. Although I don't have any details, I wonder why they were always in such turmoil. I also was curious about their self-esteem, morale, productivity, etc. Employees who are this upset usually do not produce quality work.

In another company, an employee told me that she had a cramp in her leg and had to see the doctor. She had an inflamed nerve which prevented her from sitting for long periods. At times, the pain was so great, she had to stand up and walk around the office.

One afternoon, the manager was leaving for the day. She asked the employee how her leg was feeling. The worker replied, "It still hurts. I had to walk around the office again." The employer chuckled, "I would have liked to have seen that." The only response the employee could muster was "Thanks a lot." The manager said, "Oh, I hope your leg is okay."

The manager should not have made the remark concerning the employee's leg or joked about her having to walk around the office. She was in pain and did not think that the remark was appropriate, in good taste, or funny. It also showed the manager's lack of consideration and respect. Aside from that, her comments showed she did not think before she spoke.

Most of the people with whom I have discussed this incident, agree with the employee. If the manager was genuinely concerned or thought before making the remark, she would have asked how her leg was feeling. When the worker replied, "It still hurts," the manager should have said, "I hope it feels better," at the very least. It was wrong for her to joke with the employee in this situation.

In another example, an employee told me about a review she had received. The employer had listed the worker's accomplishments and faults and then discussed the list with her. She had basically been given a good evaluation; however, all she remembered was how picky the manager was during their conversation.

However, toward the end of the review, the manager told her, "I know I'm being picky but you say too many 'ums.' If you listen when I'm on the phone, I constantly talk and I don't pause." She further stated, "You've gotten a good review. I wouldn't want you think you were perfect." The employee replied, "How could I think I was perfect since I have a lot of things I still need to accomplish?"

The manager negated the good review by being overly critical. Although she admitted she was being picky, there was no reason to tell the employee that she used too many "ums." The worker told me that she overheard several of the manager's conversations after this review. If the employer had listened to herself, she would have known she was guilty of doing the same thing. Later, I learned the manager continued to use "ums" while speaking on the phone.

In researching this book, I spoke with several managers and business owners who replied, "Oh, brother, good grief, or how petty."

At this employee's next evaluation the following year, which was also late, she received a raise but, once again, the manager negated the one positive aspect of the review. She gave the worker more money but what followed was inexcusable.

First, the manager had waited until the review to criticize the employee for something she viewed as a mistake. The worker explained that she had been given various instructions from the other managers and had acted on those instructions. This boss became sarcastic, hostile, and did not listen to anything she said. Ironically, the employer wanted to talk to her before she read it to soften the blow. However, I do not believe the manager thought she would say anything and when she did speak up in her own defense, the manager became sarcastic.

The employee had every right to discuss the incident with the manager. The employer should not have become sarcastic and hostile nor should she have waited until this employee's review to bring it to her attention. An employee should not be criticized while you are angry but any problems should be discussed with that individual without too much time elapsing.

Second, the manager told the employee that since she gave her a raise, she thought about eliminating her benefits but someone had talked her out of it. The manager never should have told the employee that she had been thinking of taking away her benefits since she had been convinced not to do so. The employer alienated the worker by mentioning it in the first place.

Third, if this was not enough, the manager told the employee she was implementing a sick-leave policy. The worker remarked that the company already had one and the amount of days due her. The manager asked her when it was implemented? She answered, "At the time of hire." The employer was going to take two days away from her but when she spoke up, the owner decided to compromise and only take away one day. Since the employee did not miss a lot of days, there was no reason for the boss to change any policy.

Fourth, the manager told the employee that she had taken too much time for doctor visits and was going to dock the time from her sick-leave days. Although she had taken more time off than usual for doctor visits for a recurring problem, which required minor surgeries, she did not miss a lot of time since it was over a period of six months. Aside from that, the employee stayed late whenever necessary and did not receive any overtime pay for staying late or for her extra efforts. She also came back to the office in spite of her major discomfort and didn't even take breaks, although by law, the employee was entitled.

The manager never considered the fact that the employee stayed late, didn't take breaks, or returned to the office after the surgeries. When the worker spoke up in her defense, the boss became sarcastic and told her she would deal with it at a later date.

After all that was said and done, the manager told the employee that if she stayed at the company another two-a-half years, she would be well-taken care of at that time.

The assistant felt it was not worthwhile anymore and decided against staying. She left the company shortly thereafter. The manager had alienated a good employee.

After learning of this incident, I discussed it with several people. They agreed with the employee's decision to leave the company. However, one person mentioned that all companies do that. Although many executives may choose to follow this path for various reasons, it does not make it right. The employee deserved to be treated better. Nonetheless, as in this example, employees are often alienated due to the management's lack of consideration, common sense and/or ethics.

In another company, an employee told me that she was scolded like a child over a mistake. The details have since been forgotten; however, in my opinion, there is no reason for an employee to be treated like a child in any situation.

In a different organization, one employer pushed his employees so hard that they eventually quit. Not only that, he didn't seem to really care or respect the people who worked for him.

One day, the supervisor in the above-mentioned company had the flu. As sick as he was, he came into the office sneezing and coughing. He did not cover his nose or mouth. One of the other employees caught it from him. Because a major project needed to be completed, she also came in sick. She barely could function but did her best and managed to complete the task.

Instead of appreciating her loyalty, the owner made a snide remark and told her to hurry up and work faster. Aside from that, the employee worked harder and could do one particular thing better than two of the newer employees who were making almost double her salary.

Eventually, the employee became upset and asked for more money. The employer did not want to increase her salary until one of the managers persisted. Reluctantly, the employer agreed. However, by that time, it was too late.

Shortly thereafter, the employee started the exodus from the company. Good employees quit in the ensuing months. When the owner was out of town, and after reviewing the year's events, the worker decided she did not want to wait. She handed in her letter of resignation to the supervisor who gave it to his boss when he returned. He asked why she didn't wait and said that he wanted to talk to her. She told him that it was a little late for talking, and he should have previously discussed her dissatisfaction. If he realized that his words and/or actions (i.e. making a snide remark or pushing his people too hard) were driving his employees away, he would not have let his best ones leave for greener pastures.

In another example, an employee had to order some items. Several times, she asked the department manager if the intended pick-up dates were okay or if more time should be given. She always answered the dates were fine. One day, the assistant had to confirm the order with the company. Someone stated more time was needed in the future. She told the employer what was said. The manager told her to give them the extra time for pick-ups and not make the company think it was a major hassle processing the orders.

The employee told me how frustrated she was. After hearing her story, I can understand her feelings. She gave the manager the information concerning the dates. At that time, the manager should have replied there was a problem instead of saying everything was fine. The employee, who was not at fault, had asked her boss twice if the dates were okay and she said yes. Therefore, the employer did not take responsibility. By telling her not to make ordering a major hassle, the manager had placed the problem on the employee's shoulders. Ironically, by asking if more time was necessary, the assistant was trying to prevent it from becoming a huge issue. Aside from that, if she said anything to her boss regarding approval of the dates, it would have made the situation worse.

In still another example, an employer reprimanded an employee for the following incident: She was waiting to send some information packets to various people, although one was held for pick-up. Several attempts were made to reach the person. Since contact was never established, the employer told her to mail that item to someone else and save another one. However, after the worker had mailed it, the individual who was previously supposed to come into the office called and said she would pick it up. The assistant inadvertently said that she would be receiving another packet instead. The employee mentioned the incident to the manager who criticized her for saying anything and told her whatever was said should have remained in the office.

The worker was upset, not at the criticism itself, but because in the past the manager had betrayed her trust by humiliating her and by not keeping two of their conversations private. Yet, she became angry when the employee said something and continued her low key tirade against the worker.

The employee told her prior to the incident that the package was going to be picked up several times and it never was. The employer was overly concerned that the packet would not be picked up and blamed the assistant. Eventually everything was fine and the individual stopped by and obtained the item. (Story was edited to provide anonymity for the employee and the company.)

Aside from that, all the manager should have told the employee is, "I wish you hadn't said what you did" and then logically explained the reasons. She did not have to lecture her especially since, in my opinion, her previous words and actions in which she betrayed the employee's confidence were far worse than what the worker supposedly did to her.

In several companies, employees were told if they missed x number of days from work, they would either be disciplined, written up, put on probation, and eventually fired.

Threatening employees with the loss of their jobs if they take what management considers too many sick days per year (i.e. more than four or six), contributes to low morale and the ill health of others. It can also add to a decline in the health of an already sick individual, if he or she can't rest and take care of himself or herself. It can also increase the person's stress levels since he or she has to decide between staying home and getting better or the possibility of losing his or her job.

If you are a manager and want to stop possible abuses, find other ways. Be creative. Think about possible positive reinforcement so that employees stay home when they are ill and come in when they are in good health. Penalizing all workers for taking care of themselves or for thinking of others will eventually cause major problems within the company.

In one company, an employee was leaving for vacation. The day before, the manager told her she would be in the office but that she had to run errands. She said that was the last day for her to do so since she would feel like a prisoner in the office. The worker said, "Thanks a lot." The employer replied, "Just kidding." Was she? The assistant knew the boss did not like being in the office. All kidding aside, she was feeling very stressed out, tired and glad to be going on vacation. It is very difficult for anyone to have a sense of humor when he or she is feeling exhausted and worrying about paying for the vacation so desperately needed.

Should the manager have said anything in the first place? Perhaps she was just being honest. However, she needed to use diplomacy and tact or think about what she was going to say before she said it.

In my opinion, the manager should have listened to the employee's concerns, realized how tired this worker was and should not have said anything.

In one company, one of the managers forced his employees to stay and finish a job during the Los Angeles riots which were two blocks away from the office. The next day, when most companies gave their staff time off, this particular boss made everyone come into work. The employer forced the workers to finish printing a newsletter for a country club of which he was also a member.

Everyone was inconvenienced by the riots and concerned for their personal safety. The job could have waited a few extra days. The employees' well-being was more important. No job is worth someone's life. Although it didn't happen, someone could have been hurt or killed going to and from work. Aside from that, the situation increased their levels of stress. By forcing the staff to come into an office, which was close to the riots, showed that the employer did not respect his employees or care about their safety.

In another company, one boss was quite particular. One evening, he was on the phone when he received another call. Since he did not like being disturbed, the employee took the information. Because it was quitting time and the company did not want to pay overtime, the worker wrote the message down and put it in the designated mailbox near his office. In the morning, the note was still there so the employee handed it to him. He then criticized her for not giving him the message the night before.

In this example, the boss was being inconsistent. He told the employee he didn't want to be disturbed while he was on the phone and then when she didn't, he criticized her for not giving him the message. As an employer, if you tell your staff not to disturb you, pay overtime. Aside from that, the boss canceled everyone's medical benefits due to budgetary constraints but had the company pay his. If you don't pay overtime or treat your employees in this manner, don't expect someone to stand around on his or her own time and wait 15 or 30 minutes until you get off the phone. In this case, since it was quitting time, the employee did the next best thing by putting the message in his box. The boss should have checked his box on his way out as well as the way into his office the next morning.

I've heard stories of employers walking around drinking coffee, taking extra time off, expecting their employees to hold their hand and/or do everything for them. Managers should be able to check their own message box especially when they tell their workers not to disturb them if they are on the phone and before or after normal business hours.

Because this next example actually falls into several categories, I have decided to mention it in this chapter to drive home a point. It is that important. Do not nitpick unless, of course, you want to alienate your employees. A lot of bosses do so without realizing that is exactly what they are doing.

This example will show that the owner is not only obsessed with perfection, but that she did not respect the employee by nitpicking. In a small company, administrative employees had to put stamps on outgoing mail since there were no postage machine or mail room personnel to handle this task. Several times, the manager mentioned that the stamps were on crooked and also made sarcastic remarks about them. In one specific incident, a boss told an employee, "You will put the stamps and labels on straight this time."

I talked to several bosses and employees and, unfortunately, in some companies, managers are that fussy. I am not advocating sloppy work habits, but when a worker, because of employer neglect, crams in seven hours of work in two and a-half hours, there will be mistakes. If the employee has to line up the stamps with the edge of the envelope to make sure they are totally straight, something more important might not be accomplished. Putting labels or stamps on crooked should not be a deal breaker. If it is, it means the receiving company is also obsessed with perfection and very petty. If crooked stamps or labels are the smallest mistakes an employee makes, don't be sarcastic and treat the individual like he or she is a child.

In Chapter Two, I mentioned several examples of managers not taking responsibility for their own actions. Since this is a very important point, other incidents pertaining to this issue will discussed in this chapter as well.

In one company, an employee worked for several supervisors who were related. One day she gave a message to one of the managers (A) who told her what to do and she, following that advice, did what was told. When the second manager (B) called in, the worker also gave her the message. B was upset at both A for not taking care of business and the employee for not giving the information to A, although the assistant said that she did so.

The next day A told B that the employee misunderstood and that she never specifically mentioned that one phone call. The worker told me that she gave that message to A who became confused. However, rather than argue with both bosses, the employee told them that she must be losing it.

The employers should not have put the employee in the middle. Instead, they needed to take responsibility and not jump to conclusions.

In another example, a manager blamed an employee for something that was not her fault. The employer was on the phone when another call had been received. In order to get her attention, the worker had attached a note with the full name of the person to a file the department already had on the individual, placed it on the desk in front of the manager and pointed to it. The boss acknowledged the information.

The manager concluded the first call and took the second. The employer, who did not look at the message, answered the phone very casually. She had thought the person was someone else. The manager explained the error by telling the caller that the employee had only given her the first name.

The manager blamed the employee for something that was not her fault. She was not paying attention and should have looked at the information before taking the second call. It would have only taken a split second and saved everyone some grief. However since that didn't happen, the manager could have just said I'm sorry or admitted that she thought the individual was someone else and apologized.

In another company, a boss intimidated an employee by telling her that she would lose her job because she didn't have the qualifications she thought she did. However, as it turned out, the boss was fired and the worker assumed his supervisory position which lasted five years.

First, show your employees respect and don't intimidate them. Second, don't threaten employees. There are better ways to handle those situations. Threatening workers increases their levels of stress. You will lose respect if your threats have no basis in fact. It is also possible, as it was in this case, that the manager making the threat would lose his own job. Remember, it only takes an extra minute to think before you speak. Choose your words carefully to not intimidate or alienate your employees. Think about it!

In another company, a boss constantly yelled at her employees for making mistakes, never complimented them for a job well done, had not given them raises in years, eliminated their medical and other benefits, and told them they could no longer receive personal phone calls.

Granted, the company was not doing well financially but the boss should have, at least, complimented the employees when they did a good job. They did not feel appreciated. Morale was at an all-time low. Why? The employer screamed at the staff for making mistakes. Workers were also upset because the boss received personal phone calls, and they could not under any circumstances. The owner was unfair because she should not have been receiving personal calls and was setting a bad example for the employees. What happened to management by example? It is more important than most managers believe.

In one company, a boss placed an employee he didn't like in the middle between himself and his valued associate who made changes on some equipment used in the department. The manager asked everyone who had changed the settings on the equipment. However, the associate would either forget and/or deny that he did so. After he denied everything, the boss would berate the other employee and made quasi-physical threats toward the end of this worker's term of the employment.

In this particular example, the employee was placed in the middle, constantly blamed for things that were not his fault, and the associate would not take responsibility for his actions. Aside from that, there was no reason to threaten anyone for his or her actions and/or words.

In another company, the owners constantly patronized their employees and were condescending toward them.

Employers want employees to take responsibility for their actions and be accountable for their mistakes. However, they also need to take responsibility for errors and not blame staff for their own shortcomings.

Let's examine the example listed below and the consequences of not taking responsibility.

An employee ordered an item from one of the company's vendors. The item was not shipped and the supply was dwindling to the point that it caused problems.

Management blamed and screamed at the employee for this incident, although she didn't do anything wrong. Later, she learned the owners had not immediately paid the vendor. The worker mentioned this to another individual who remarked, "If you ordered it and followed up when you were supposed to, why are they screaming at and blaming you, when it's not your fault?"

How do you think that employee felt after being blamed for something that was not her fault? Of course, she is going to feel angry and frustrated especially after the employer lectured and screamed at her. Telling another employee about what happened shows she was angry and upset. Once you've angered, frustrated, and alienated your worker, expect morale and productivity to plummet. The longer and more often you blame or scream at the staff for your own shortcomings, the faster morale will decrease and the easier it will be for the employee to quit.

I find it ironic that these owners wanted the employees to take responsibility for their errors, etc. However, they made it difficult for the workers to admit their mistakes. In other words, they yelled and became sarcastic. Aside from that, by not taking responsibility, they did not set an example for the employees and demonstrated a lack of respect.

A better way is to take responsibility, be honest and then discuss the situation with the employee. One example could be, "We blew it. The item isn't here because we didn't send the payment when it was ordered." Although the best way was to not blame her at all but once they did, they should have apologized. They didn't and that was why the worker was so upset.

One of the owners told an employee, "We can be rude to each other but be nice to customers." The workers hated being treated in that manner but they were too afraid to speak up. However, one day, an owner wrote a memo to the staff. It said, "Be logical, Think," and an assortment of other comments. Under a veil of anonymity, the employees struck back, writing a number of comments on the correspondence, which included, "You don't pay us enough, stop insulting our intelligence, don't jump to conclusions until you have all the facts," etc.

The employer also made statements which were not conducive to increasing morale. She thought a particular employee said that she wasn't being paid enough. The owner jumped to conclusions and said, "We gave you a raise. We're giving you a liveable wage. By the time we pay for all of your mistakes, we're making the same amount of money."

While this might be the truth from the employer's point of view, what did she hope to accomplish by making that comment? It wasn't to increase morale. Aside from that, $8.00 an hour is hardly a liveable wage in today's economy and if an employee believes he or she isn't getting paid enough to begin with, that in itself decreases morale. Sometimes, employers don't "get it."

Employee discontent had been brewing for awhile and the memo only added fuel to the fire. Worker morale plummeted and negativity increased.

The employers took the staff to lunch the next day but that didn't resolve the issues because they didn't change their behavior. The condescending and patronizing attitudes and the screaming and yelling continued. Attitude, pay, and benefits motivate people, not lunches. The owners did not believe that attitude came from the top and trickled down. People cannot change unless they are ready to do so. When employers are in denial, change will not happen. Saying that everyone could be rude to each other did not help an already negative situation. It made things worse. Where's the logic and common sense in the statement, "We can be rude to each other but be nice to customers?" There isn't! The employers wondered why people had attitudes. It's obvious.

The employers continued to be condescending and patronizing. Did employees speak up? Yes, but it did not do any good. As time flew by, the situation escalated. One of the owners began to yell and scream at employees if they made mistakes, didn't clean up, or put merchandise away fast enough, etc. It wasn't a one time lecture or screaming session that was directed at the employees, the verbal attacks and/or lectures continued for minutes and many times for an hour or two.

One day, however, the situation escalated again. This time, one of the owners became furious at an employee for not putting merchandise away fast enough, although she was trying to send out as many orders as possible and a co-worker was running company errands.

First, the owner screamed at the employee, literally shoved and kicked boxes out the door, and then walked over to a table two feet from the employee and punched a box while continuing her tirade. Two other employees witnessed the box incident and the verbal attack and another only witnessed the verbal tirade.

Second, the next day, the other owner called the employee into the office and closed the door so there would be no witnesses.

She blamed her for the incident, the negativity, and said they could treat the employees any way they wanted, that employer/employee relations had nothing to do with anything, and to change her attitude or quit. The worker decided to quit and file an unemployment claim instead of going out on stress since she was one month shy of eligibility.

Upon quitting, the employee received a lot of validation because it was a very hostile environment. She had every right to feel frustrated, angry and threatened. During discussions with social workers, a psychologist, and several doctors, they all agreed that she was correct in quitting and had great cause—her safety and well-being. The chief of police of the city in which the event occurred couldn't do anything because she wasn't hit. However, a senator, an assemblymember, and various employees of Cal-OSHA believed her.

The employers fought the unemployment claim and one told the judge under oath that she never yelled, screamed, shoved, kicked boxes out the door or punched a box two feet from the employee. The employer further mentioned that the worker made it up because she could not find a job and needed the money. The owner stated that the "other boss" would not have told her, "We can treat employees any way we want."

Later, the former employee wanted to see her file even though she quit and was not fired. The employer answered her request but instead of July 13, 2000, the date on the letter was June 13, 2000. An honest mistake or manipulation? The boss repeatedly said at the unemployment and labor commission hearings that the worker had a bad attitude and everyone had complained about it. If that was the case, why wasn't there any documentation in her file? The employee told me there was nothing in it. Aside from that, the employer who spoke to the worker on December 16, 1999, left a message on her machine saying, "Nothing you've done makes any sense."

I don't agree. Everything the employee did made sense. Her last day was December 16, 1999 and she was entitled to receive pay for December 14-16, 1999. They made her wait until the next pay period for the balance of her salary instead of the 72 hours as required by law. She wasn't going to do anything until they fought her unemployment insurance claim and denied the truth under oath. She filed a complaint with the labor commission in her state for waiting time penalties. There was more concrete evidence but there was a different pay period on the check stub. Instead of November 30, 1999 to December 13, 1999, the check stub stated December 3, 1999 to December 16, 1999. How ingenious!

This is not the situation you want to create in your workplace or even after an employee quits. It can have very negative consequences.

CA law states employers are to provide a "safe and healthful" environment. According to Roget's Thesaurus, safe means "free from danger, injury, or the threat of harm." Healthful doesn't only mean clean. Synonyms include: salutary, beneficial, benevolence, humane, and kindness. Therefore, by definition, the work environment was not safe and healthful. There were also roaches crawling all over the dishes in the kitchen.

CA Labor Code 6306a Safety and Health states, "Safe as applied to an employment or place of employment means such freedom from danger to the life, safety, or health of employees as the nature of the employment reasonably permits." Because of the ambiguity of Cal-OSHA's guidelines and the labor code, the codes should have been applied to the situation I described.

While researching this book, I spoke to an employee at the CA Department of Industrial Relations office in San Francisco. He told me there was no code covering workplace violence. I found that very interesting.

I concur with the labor code and the guidelines, which were written as a common sense approach to management. However, Cal-OSHA is only an investigative agency. They have no enforcement power, as I've been told. Cal-OSHA's health, safety, and labor codes should be enforced for the well-being of all employees. Its guidelines state that government "can't do it alone."

However, if some employers do not believe that their attitudes affect morale, productivity, customer service, etc., they are not going to believe that their attitudes can influence employee behavior concerning hostility, sabotage, and violence.

I know it is not easy to admit you have a problem or take responsibility for your actions but if you find yourself losing control, as the owner did in the above example, do yourself and your employees a favor. GET HELP!

It's a fine line between hitting something and someone. Within one week after the employee left, she learned the situation had escalated again. This time the boss threw a plastic bin and hit a worker in the back.

According to Cal-OSHA's guidelines, "Some mental health experts believe that belligerent, intimidating, or threatening behavior is an early warning sign of an individual's propensity to commit a physical assault in the future."

Intimidating, threatening, or hitting your employees is counter productive, decreases morale, productivity, customer service, and eventually your bottom line. Turnover is expensive.

However, there are more important reasons to treat your workers with consideration and respect. According to Cal-OSHA's guidelines, consideration and respect by an employer can help prevent violence in the workplace. I agree. There are also other negative effects. Sabotage and theft, to name only two. I'm not saying that it's right for employees to act in this manner. It isn't. Personal responsibility issues need to be addressed. Unfortunately, events can and do happen when people feel they are backed into a corner and have nothing to lose.

I would like to suggest that if you are an employee in a hostile environment, get help from an Employee Assistance Program (EAP) if the company has one or go outside the organization for counseling if it doesn't. You can also write to your local assemblymembers, senators, and governor, etc. Let them know what is going on. If they do not know what's happening in your workplace, they cannot fix it.

This is the 21st century, not the dark ages of employment. Situations such as I described should not be happening today. There are laws and they need to be enforced. Investigation is not enough. Do employees and employers have to get hurt because the government won't do anything or because employers and employees can't take personal or general responsibility? Workplace violence is a serious occupational health and safety hazard. Isn't it time we all did our part to prevent workplace violence?

Above all, remember, if you feel you are losing control, get help. It's the best thing you can do for yourself, your employees, co-workers, and your peers. I can't stress these and the following points enough! Take responsibility for your own actions.

Do not blame your employee for something that is not his/her fault. Do not place your worker in the middle. Apologize when you are wrong. Think before you speak. Listen to complaints and suggestions. Allow employees to complain without fear of recrimination. Be a diplomat. If you have to be firm, at least be diplomatic, considerate, and respectful. These measures just might help prevent violence or sabotage in the workplace.

Managers seem to think that admitting to a mistake is a sign of weakness. I happen to disagree. It takes a big person to admit responsibility and say I'm sorry or I apologize. Blaming your employee when it isn't his/her fault is also frustrating and increases stress levels.

There is also no logic or common sense when employers destroy trust and teamwork within the ranks. Trust, teamwork, and cooperation are also vital to the success of an organization. Instead of building trust and a team spirit, managers, owners, supervisors, and co-workers can and do consciously and subconsciously destroy them. This "divide and conquer" mentality is harmful to the work environment because it causes friction between employees.

Employers can destroy trust between workers by telling another employee that "everyone is talking about his/her attitude." It doesn't matter if everyone is talking about a certain individual or whether or not he/she has a bad attitude especially if all the workers have negative attitudes. The more important issue which needs to be addressed is that the employer is turning employees against each other.

Turning employees against each other causes friction within the ranks. Employers' careless statements do nothing more than add fuel to the fire and turn employees into uncaring workers who resent and no longer trust each other. Bosses who cause problems can "kiss" team spirit, trust, and cooperation goodbye.

Instead, when discussing a negative situation with an employee, leave the comments of co-workers out of the equation. Statements such as, "everyone says you have a bad attitude," or "everyone is talking about you" do not show common sense. They are also not constructive forms of criticism and accomplish nothing positive.

There are better ways of handling these type of situations. When employers don't behave ethically, I have to ask will bosses ever learn how to treat their employees? I certainly hope they learn it is okay to treat their subordinates as human beings.

And now on to Chapter Twelve, "Do Managers Really Know How to Manage?"

CHAPTER TWELVE

"DO MANAGERS REALLY KNOW

HOW TO MANAGE?"

"THE FINAL CHAPTER"

If you've read this book in its entirety, you are already aware that the answer is yes and no.

Unfortunately there are a lot of bosses who should not be in positions of authority and cannot handle situations or deal effectively with people. However, some employers really do know how to manage and are quite adept at handling issues that may arise. They have "people skills" and treat employees as human beings.

Contrary to what most people may think, treating employees as human beings and validating their feelings are strengths, not weaknesses. If you are having a bad day, don't take it out on your staff. I know it's not always easy having a great attitude when you don't feel like it. Your employees might be going through personal crises as well, ranging from domestic violence problems to caregiving issues. Proper communication is important. Attitude comes from the top and employees will follow your cue. However, depending on the problem, sometimes all it takes to resolve an issue is to recognize and validate the person's feelings.

Bosses tell employees do not take my mood swings to heart, leave your personal problems at the door, and lose the negative attitudes. One worker mentioned a supervisor told her to leave her problems at home. However, in reality in this case, her problems stemmed from the manager who drove everyone crazy, and was actually the one who should have left her problems at the door. How ironic!

In today's workplace, employees have too many outside stresses. The concept of leaving your problems at the door is great but not feasible. Employers have to "manage" the entire person because he or she is human and has feelings and emotions that cannot and should not be separated from that individual.

Giving an employee a bonus or raise is great. However, constantly blaming someone for things he/she did not do, being overly critical if the individual makes a mistake, or mistreating your people throughout the year negates the positive accomplishments.

Remember that some employees also deal with customers. As managers, business owners, or company officers, you may want to think twice about mistreating your staff. How do you expect an employee to be sympathetic to a customer's needs or handle a complaint after he or she has just been humiliated, screamed at for making a mistake, criticized at every turn, or given added responsibilities without any kind of compensation or respect? You shouldn't!

Some managers may think I am overly picky and perhaps I am being too critical. However, some people need to be told several times that their words and/or actions can have negative effects. Of course, no matter how many times managers and employers are told that their words and/or actions could be responsible for the loss of their best staff, or worse, they won't listen or accept responsibility for the problems they cause.

Some managers or owners who feel stress because a client is in town or have a lot of phone calls to make, can assign duties and leave the premises to relax.

Employees also feel stress but can't delegate work and/or responsibility and are not allowed to take time from the job. They are also told to prioritize and not become overwhelmed when they are given more tasks. If workers feel unrewarded (financial or otherwise), any additional projects will add to their anxieties. Aside from that, due to downsizing and the threat of unemployment, they are also concerned about their jobs, their futures, feeding their families, and/or making ends meet. Loyalty and job security are things that don't exist in most companies any more.

In California, employment is "at will." Basically, that means an employer can terminate an employee with or without cause. In many companies, workers are considered liabilities, not assets. If you've hired the right people and you're good to them, they'll be good to you. Loyalty is a two way street.

Employees also have to try and please their bosses, which in itself, is very stressful. For some owners, it doesn't matter if a worker is doing his or her best, he or she has to be perfect. An employer can say and do anything he/she wants and if the individual makes a mistake, it's okay. Right? No! This adds more stress to an already anxious employee. Imagine how an individual would feel if he or she was sarcastically reprimanded for making a mistake and later, the person saw a letter that the boss typed and mailed containing several errors. He or she would be upset. If you are sarcastic and become defensive, you will also be contributing to your subordinate's stress level.

Employers in California are complaining about the high cost of workers' compensation claims. However if those in authority realized that if they treated their employees with respect and consideration, it may just lessen the amount of stress claims and produce more positive results within the company. Perhaps, it is time for employers to take a good hard look at themselves.

If you only remember one of the points discussed in this book, remember to treat people the way you would like to be treated. If you don't like being humiliated, screamed at, or blamed for something you didn't do, etc., then do not do it to someone else.

On the other hand, if you like being mistreated or feel employees are subservient and it is okay to mistreat them, it is time to take a long hard look at yourself and change your way of thinking. You might just be surprised at the results.

In closing, here are a few points to remember. "Attitude" starts at the top and "trickles" down. Work together not against each other.

Remember, you can keep employees happy without "giving away the store." However, no matter who you are (employee, supervisor, manager, or owner), if you start to lose control, get help! It is the ethical and moral thing to do!

If this book changes management's perceptions of employer/employee relations, I will have accomplished my objective; improving the relationship between employers and employees.

www.ingramcontent.com/pod-product-compliance
Lightning Source LLC
Chambersburg PA
CBHW030906180526
45163CB00004B/1730